Focused Leadership

Focused Leadership

*Instruction, Learning,
and School Improvement*

Roger E. Jones

Rowman & Littlefield
Lanham • Boulder • New York • London

Published by Rowman & Littlefield
A wholly owned subsidiary of The Rowman & Littlefield Publishing Group, Inc.
4501 Forbes Boulevard, Suite 200, Lanham, Maryland 20706
www.rowman.com

16 Carlisle Street, London W1D 3BT, United Kingdom

Copyright © 2014 by Roger E. Jones

All rights reserved. No part of this book may be reproduced in any form or by any electronic or mechanical means, including information storage and retrieval systems, without written permission from the publisher, except by a reviewer who may quote passages in a review.

British Library Cataloguing in Publication Information Available

Library of Congress Cataloging-in-Publication Data

978-1-4758-1033-2 (cloth : alk. paper)
978-1-4758-1034-9 (pbk. : alk. paper)
978-1-4758-1035-6 (electronic)

∞^{TM} The paper used in this publication meets the minimum requirements of American National Standard for Information Sciences—Permanence of Paper for Printed Library Materials, ANSI/NISO Z39.48-1992.

Printed in the United States of America

Contents

Introduction	vii
Chapter One Planning	1
Chapter Two Learning Theory	7
Chapter Three Differentiation, Learning Styles, and Thinking Taxonomy	11
Chapter Four The Lesson Line	15
Chapter Five Research-Based Instructional Strategies	17
Chapter Six Practice and Retention	23
Chapter Seven Reinforcement and Intangibles	27
Chapter Eight Student Engagement	33
Chapter Nine Formative Assessment	41
Chapter Ten The Essential Twelve	45
Chapter Eleven Five Levels of Listening and Qualities of Effective Feedback	55
Chapter Twelve The School Improvement Process	59
Chapter Thirteen Creating a Culture of Achievement	65
Chapter Fourteen Instruction and Learning	69
Chapter Fifteen Expanding the Leadership Capacity of Others	77
Chapter Sixteen Establishing Cultural Change and Rebranding	83
Chapter Seventeen Final Thoughts	87
References and Further Readings	91
About the Author	95

Introduction

Focused Learning: Instruction, Learning, and School Improvement

Building level and central office administrators must be both instructional and learning leaders. Although these terms are often used interchangeably, for the purpose of this document, they should be thought about as separate but related terms. Instructional leadership means focusing on teacher behaviors that support student learning and helping teachers make good decisions about their own behaviors in the teaching process.

On the other hand, learning leadership focuses on the actual learning itself, how students absorb, process, and retain information. This focus requires an understanding of the conceptual frameworks of learning theories. Teachers must teach in a manner that maximizes learning, that is, they must make good decisions about their own behaviors (instructional leadership) *around* an understanding of how students learn (learning leadership).

To help teachers become better at both instructional and learning leadership, building level and central office administrators need to be coaches for their teachers. Just as it is an athletic coach's responsibility to make athletes better players, the same is true for administrators and their teachers. Some administrators argue there is not enough time to do this; however, the truth is that administrators do not have the time to neglect this vital responsibility. People can always find time to do what is important, and so administrators must find the time to be both instructional and learning leaders.

> Focus on what is important. If everything is important, nothing is important. Instructional and learning leadership are important!

There are two ways to improve schools: replace current teachers with teachers who are better or help current teachers become more effective. Generally, in each school there are superstar teachers, teachers who are master craftsmen at what they do. There are also a few teachers who should not be teaching. If efforts to help these teachers grow do not help, they should be counseled out of the profession or escorted to the door.

The future of a school, however, is determined by what happens with the average teachers, those teachers between the bottom 10 percent and the superstars. Do they start to look like the bottom 10 percent or do they start to look more like superstars? The job of an administrator coach is to help them become more like the superstars.

The visual model, "Instructional and Learning Leadership: The Interconnection of Teaching and Learning," provides the foundation for the discussion of instructional and learning leadership. It is a guide to assist administrators in their quest to be more effective at what they do, not a prescriptive document, but rather a baseline from which to grow. The model is a result of more than thirty years of trying to figure out the teaching and learning process. It has been changed many times and influenced by many people. The model is presented as a global look at many of the elements that relate to teacher behaviors and student learning.

The visual model presents a view from 30,000 feet while this guide goes to ground level in discussing the importance of each element included in the model. The model is not designed to overwhelm principals or teachers; however, all educators need to be aware of the intricacy of the teaching and learning process and how all elements are linked. The model provides a foundation for observations and conversations about both instructional and learning leadership. Teachers could never be expected to demonstrate every element of the model during a lesson, nor should anyone ever want them to.

Educators are encouraged to use the visual model as a foundation, as a starting point to expand instructional and learning leadership. They should modify the model, add to it, and personalize it as they challenge themselves to grow. What is important is that educators take instructional and learning leadership seriously. They must see themselves as transformational leaders and change agents. Great educators transform schools.

The visual model encompasses many components, all of which are important and are described along with additional information with some connection to research. The model should help administrators to know what to look for during an observation, and, perhaps even more impor-

> If your actions inspire others to dream more, learn more, do more, and become more, you are a leader.
>
> John Quincy Adams

Instructional and Learning Leadership: The Interconnection of Teaching and Learning © Roger Jones 2013

PLANNING
- Data Analysis (know every student)
- Student Profile
- Curriculum Framework
- Pacing Guide
- Academic Rigor
- Lesson Plan
- Examples of "A" Work
- Room Configuration
- Acceleration
- Materials (varied/leveled)
- Connection to Vision
- High Expectations
- Study Skills/ Learning Strategies
- Knowledge, Problem Solving, Concepts

Differentiation
- Curriculum
  • Content
  • Process
  • Product
- Student
  • Readiness
  • Interest
  • Learning Profile

Learning Styles
- Auditory
- Visual
- Tactual
- Kinesthetic
- Global
- Analytic

Thinking Taxonomy
- Knowledge
- Comprehension
- Application
- Analysis
- Synthesis
- Evaluation

Learning Theory
- Behaviorist
- Cognitivist
- Humanist
- Constructivist
- Experientialist
- Contextual

Monitor and Adjust

Teacher					Objective
Lesson Frame	Method of Delivery	Activity	Thoughtful Extension (Cultivate Curiosity & Inquiry)		

Research-Based Instructional Strategies
- Similarities and Differences
- Summarizing and Notetaking
- Homework and Practice
- Nonlinguistic Representation
- Generating and Testing Hypotheses
- Cues, Questions, Advance Organizers
- Interactive Notebook
- Jigsaw
- Graphic Organizers
- Word Walls
- Manipulatives
- Inside/Outside Circle
- Metacognition (Student Awareness of Own Thinking – Goals, Self-Monitoring, Self-Predicting, Paraphrasing, Questioning)

Practice
- Guided
- Independent
- Massed
- Distributed

Retention
- Relevance
- Original Learning

Reinforcement
- Positive
- Negative
- Extinction

Intangibles
- Eye Contact
- Expression/Tone
- Movement
- Personalization
- Motivation
- Relationships

Student Engagement
- Behavioral Engagement
  • Expectations
  • Structure
  • Attention
  • Accountability
- Cognitive Engagement
  • Learning Goals
  • Challenging
  • Success
  • Active
  • Creativity
  • Probing
  • Wait Time
  • Accountability
  • Responsible for Learning
  • Level of Questions
  • Grouping (pairs/small/large)
- Emotional Engagement
  • Effort
  • Persistence
  • Quality of Work
  • Delight in Accomplishment
  • Growth Mindset

Formative Assessment Strategies
- Pre/Post Tests
- Feedback Connected to Learning
- Level of Questions
- Checking Notebooks/Journals
- Checking Homework
- Rough Drafts
- Think/Pair/Share
- Clickers
- Exit Tickets
- Thinking/Concept/Web Maps
- Three Minute Paper
- One Minute Summary
- Quiz/Test
- Rubrics
- Reflections

Formative Assessment Evidence of Use
- Adapt Teaching to Student Needs
- Re-Teach/Enrichment/Acceleration
- Verbal/Written Feedback
- Referral for Intervention
- Re-Group
- Model How Work Can Be Improved
- Student Must Act on Feedback

This framework is influenced by the work of Madeline Hunter, Bob Marzano, Rita Dunn, Carol Tomlinson, Benjamin Bloom, Sam Redding, Richard and Becky DuFour, Mike DiPaola, Carol Dweck, John Hattie, Bob Crane, Breaking Ranks®, and the National Institute of School Leadership (NISL).

Figure I.1.

YOU ARE A TRANSFORMATIONAL LEADER AND CHANGE AGENT!

The Essential 12

- Educators must be instructional and learning leaders.
- Effort and persistence lead to increased learning.
- Great teaching matters.
- Learning takes time but must lead to college and career ready graduates.
- High expectations promote learning.
- Vision, non-negotiables, and intentionality create a trifecta for success.
- Growth mindsets are a foundation for increased student learning.
- Motivation matters, intrinsic motivation matters more.
- Tight alignment of curriculum, instruction, and assessment makes a difference.
- Feedback must stimulate action.
- Every child, by need, every day.
- Educators must be transformational leaders.

Five Levels of Listening

- Ignoring
- Pretending
- Selective
- Attentive
- Empathic

Qualities of Effective Feedback

- Intended to help
- Your interpretation
- Delivered in the moment
- Presumes that the teacher wants to improve
- Describes behavior
- Open ended v. directive questions
- Authentic/candid
- 3-Deep questioning
- Stimulates action

Bibliography

Bloom, Benjamin (1984). *Taxonomy of Educational Objectives*. Longman: White Plains, NY.

Cain, Sean and Mike Laird (2011). *The Fundamental 5: The Formula for Quality Instruction*. Self-Published.

Covey, Stephen (1990). *The 7 Habits of Highly Effective People*. New York: Free Press.

Crane, Thomas G. (2012). *The Heart of Coaching*. FTA Press: San Diego, CA.

DiPaola, Michael (2007). *Principals Improving Instruction: Supervision, Evaluation, and Professional Development*. Allyn and Bacon: Boston.

DuFour, Richard (2008). *Revisiting Professional Learning Communities at Work: New Insights for Improving Schools*. Solution Tree: Bloomington, ILL.

Dunn, Rita (1993). *Teaching Secondary Students Through Their Individual Learning Styles*. Allyn and Bacon: Boston.

Dweck, Carol (2006). *Mindset: The New Psychology of Success*. Ballantine Books: New York.

Hattie, John (2012). *Visible Learning for Teachers*. Routledge: New York.

Hunter, Robin (2004). *Madeline Hunter's Mastery Teaching: Increasing Instructional Effectiveness in Elementary and Secondary Schools*. Corwin Press: Thousand Oaks, CA.

Marzano, Robert J. (2003). *What Works in Schools: Translating Research into Action*. ASCD: Alexandria, VA.

National Institute of School Leadership. Website at http://www.nisl.net/.

Redding, Sam (2006). *The Mega System*. Academic Development Institute: Lincoln, ILL.

Tomlinson, Carol (2010). *Leading and Managing a Differentiated Classroom*. ASCD: Alexandria, VA.

tant, topics of conversations to have with teachers. Being a change agent (transformational leader) begins with quality conversations.

In addition, principals must lead the school improvement process. While there are various models for school improvement, there are critical elements that form the foundation for creating cultural change within a building. In later chapters, there will be a discussion of these critical elements.

ONE

Planning

When educators think of planning, it is generally the lesson plan that first comes to mind. Administrators look for the lesson plan on classroom visits, and some administrators have teachers turn in lesson plans on a weekly basis. Notwithstanding the importance of lesson planning, however, the planning process includes much more. As administrators engage teachers in conversations about instruction and learning, it is important to have powerful conversations about what is important. The following aspects of planning are items for such conversations.

First, teachers need to know every student well. No matter how many students they teach, 25 or 125, teachers need to know each one of them. It is hard for teachers to teach students they do not know. Furthermore, students know when teachers make the effort to know something about them and this makes a difference, helping students connect to adults they can see themselves becoming.

> Students need to connect to an adult they can see themselves becoming.
>
> *Breaking Ranks®, NASSP*

Teachers should be able to identify every student who has failed a standards of learning (SOL) or end-of-course (EOC) assessment. Outside of Virginia, teachers should be able to identify every student who has failed a Common Core or state assessment. While state assessments should be only one measure of achievement, administrators and teachers must realize that these assessments are important.

It is also important that teachers develop a general profile of each student. Although there is no defined way to do this, there are numerous effective ways to develop the profile. For example, teachers can review the student's cumulative folder. They can also create an online survey and have students complete it in the computer lab or on classroom computers. Of course, teachers can always have students put survey information on a note card, perhaps the "old fashioned" way, but still effective. Another powerful strategy is to ask parents to share one to three things about their child that they want the teacher to know. No one knows the child like the parent, so teachers should take advantage of this valuable resource while getting to know their students.

There are other resources as well to help teachers get to know their students. For example, teachers need to explore possible resources with school counselors. In Virginia, one such resource is the Academic and Career Plan, begun in the seventh grade and reviewed and modified in both ninth and eleventh grades. This plan, developed by students and parents, provides excellent insight into students' long term goals and dreams.

Just as it is critical during the planning process for teachers to know their students, it is also vital for teachers to examine and know well the curriculum framework and division pacing guides for which they are responsible. Every school division has them, and they are all based on the state standards.

Because academic rigor is very important, it too has a prominent role in the planning process. Every teacher should be able to define academic rigor and what it means in the classroom. There is an inherent problem with this, however, as different teachers will often define academic rigor very differently, with superstar teachers and average teachers often disagreeing about what the term means.

So, a transformational administrator may need to drive the discussion of academic rigor. An excellent strategy for this discussion is one from National Association of Secondary School Principals' (NASSP) *Breaking Ranks®*. Following is a blueprint by which a school or department may develop a consistent definition of academic rigor. It is the 1-2-4-8-16-32 activity described below.

1-2-4-8-16-32 Activity

1. Have each teacher in the school or department define academic rigor.
2. Pair two teachers and have them combine their definition into one they can live with.
3. Pair two pairs and do the same thing.
4. Continue the pairing process until there is one definition for the school or department.

Once there is a school or department definition, the administrator can take the conversation to the next level by posting the definition and asking teachers to determine what curriculum, instruction, and assessment should look like with this definition of academic rigor.

Thinking prompts can also promote academic rigor and creativity. Knight (2013) defines thinking prompts as "video clips, photographs, newspaper articles, popular songs, and other devices as catalysts for discussion, dialogue, and higher order thinking" (p. 17). This strategy when used effectively by teachers can lead to rich conversations and experiences in the classroom.

Of course, the familiar lesson plan itself is part of the planning process, but teachers also need to think about ways they can share with students what "A" work looks like. Many "C," "D," and "F" students have no idea what "A" or "B" work actually looks like because they have never produced it. Some students believe they are giving the teacher what the teacher wants, but they are mistaken. Pedro Noguera from New York University, who works with large urban school divisions around the country, said that students who have never been successful do not know how to be successful unless teachers show and model success. Clarity of expectations is part of the planning process.

Clarity precedes competence.

Richard and Becky DuFour

While often overlooked, room configuration is something to think about during the planning process because appropriate configurations can promote learning. For example, for teacher-directed lessons, using the traditional rows of desks may be most effective. If students are working on their own, however, placing the desks around the perimeter of the room may be helpful. When students are learning from each other, a circle is effective; otherwise, students often do not benefit from what others say because they cannot hear them. When teachers are differentiating, a variety of seating options may be helpful.

John Hattie's (2011) research demonstrates the power of accelerating learning and of creating high expectations as part of the planning process. Students who are behind will never catch up unless they accelerate their learning or unless the people ahead of them decelerate theirs. Slowing down instruction for the top students would be ethically wrong and cannot be an option. Thus, teachers must adopt a mindset that students can learn more at a faster rate. Planning must incorporate ways to provide interventions and safety nets for students in the acceleration process.

Although it appears just a simplistic concept, creating an atmosphere of high expectations for all students is critically important. Students must be challenged to be college and career ready. Educators must talk with students about expectations, challenge them, encourage them, and motivate them to higher levels of achievement. Educators must be cheerleaders for high expectations. They must have a mindset that students will learn and grow academically. They must challenge students to give their best effort every day.

As teachers plan for instruction, they also need to focus on available materials. While this includes textbooks, it should include multiple additional learning resources for students. Teachers should plan to have and use a variety of resources as well as leveled resources that accommodate various skill proficiencies. As teachers monitor and adjust instruction, it is easier to do so if there has been some advanced thought (planning) given to what alternative resources to use if the initial resources do not work. Resources alone will not serve students well if appropriate research-based strategies are not used.

The importance of vision in the planning process cannot be overestimated. Schools and school improvement should be driven by a vision that identifies where the school wants to go, what it wants to become, and how students will be different as a result of receiving an education in that school. The greatest obstacle to school reform, according to NASSP's *Breaking Ranks®* initiative, is the lack of a compelling vision. Every teacher, every administrator, every student, and every parent should know and be committed to the vision. In the planning process, teachers need to be constantly focused on how the teaching and learning in their classroom impacts the school vision.

> Vision without action is a daydream. Action without vision is a nightmare.
>
> Japanese Proverb

For example, if the vision/mission statement is "every child, every day, by need, to graduation" (the vision/mission statement of Lynchburg, VA Public Schools), teachers must be willing to buy into and support this. They must focus on making sure that the interactions that occur on a daily basis with students support student learning and student achievement. This requires that teachers be very intentional about connecting to the vision/mission statement.

Hattie's (2011) research notes that providing students with study skills and learning strategies have high effect sizes and so this too must be part of planning. Integrating study skills and learning strategies with lessons has been shown to be more effective than teaching them independently. A great deal of research is available to teachers, but a few examples include references on how to study, importance of effort, note taking, types of study, and time management. There are specific strategies that can be used as well, e.g. SQ3R (survey, question, read, recite, review).

Planning for effective instruction also means focusing on what is important within the content. For example, good math and science instruction should emphasize three important concepts. In other words, it is like a three-legged stool. Teachers need to focus on the three legs—knowledge, problem-solving, and concepts. There must be content-focused, evidence-based teaching that encourages inquiry and connection of big ideas.

First, students have to have the knowledge—which includes vocabulary and skills—necessary for success. If students need to be able to multiply, they need to know the multiplication tables. If formulas are important, they need to understand them. Beyond knowledge, however, students must also apply, that is, use knowledge to solve problems. Finally, students have to see how concepts connect, in other words, the big picture.

Instruction that focuses on only one or two of the three elements is a disservice to students. It may also be one of the reasons math and science scores are so low in the United States compared to the scores of international students. Drilling students with facts without letting them use the facts to solve problems or to make conceptual connections is ineffective. Giving students the formulas and multiplication tables to solve problems is ineffective.

Teaching students to add, subtract, multiply, and divide without seeing conceptual connections or teaching photosynthesis without connecting the concepts of energy and respiration is ineffective. Teachers must plan to include all three aspects of three-legged stool instruction, especially as instruction relates to math and science.

Two mind frames discussed by Hattie (2011) help to provide transition to other topics in the teaching and learning process:

- Teachers/leaders believe that their fundamental task is to evaluate the effect of their teaching on students' learning and achievement.
- Teachers/leaders believe that success and failure in student learning is about what they, as teachers or leaders, did or did not do.... They see themselves as change agents!

If you always do what you've always done, you'll always get what you've always got.

—*Anonymous*

There are other elements to the planning process as well, but they will be examined as stand-alone concepts. These include differentiation, learning styles, thinking, and learning theory.

Two

Learning Theory

LEARNING THEORIES

Learning theories are conceptual frameworks describing how information is absorbed, processed, and retained. It is important for teachers to think about a variety of learning theories and consider ways to construct learning experiences and student engagement opportunities that increase the probability that students will learn and retain important information. While there are a variety of learning theories, six will be discussed here: behaviorism, cognitivism, humanism, constructivism, experientialism, and contextual.

Behaviorism

Behaviorism is based on creating behavioral changes with new behavioral patterns repeated until they become automatic. Behaviorism relies on stimulus–response: teachers provide the stimulus and students respond. Teachers develop a system of rewards and punishments to condition learning, creating targets for students and providing rewards when students meet their targets. If teachers can control the learning environment, they can change behavior.

With behaviorist theory, teachers need to complete a task analysis to identify steps in the learning process. Some refer to this as creating enabling objectives so that students can meet a standard. Learner objectives are predetermined, and teachers prescribe experiences to help students master the standards. Criterion-referenced assessments are used to evaluate students on the same standards.

Cognitivism

Cognitivism is based on the thought process behind the behavior. When changes in behavior occur, it is an indication of what is going on in the learner's head. Change in behavior is conscious and intentional. Emphasis is placed on memory, thinking, and reflection.

With this theory, teachers conduct a cognitive task analysis to determine mental operations. They ask themselves, "How will my students think about a problem?" Teachers then focus on helping students develop mental models and teaching their students how to think. They use complex problems to encourage students to think through the process, make connections, and solve the problem. As with behaviorism, criterion-referenced assessments are used to measure progress.

Humanism

Humanism is based on the theory that learning results from the need to express creativity. It maintains that students need a creative outlet and must engage in creative activity in order to gain a sense of control, growth, and knowledge. This learning theory accepts that students have an inner drive that encourages learning and expression. With this theory, the teacher is more of a facilitator than instructor, and students take more control over the learning process.

Teachers negotiate objectives with students in a humanistic classroom and analyze the tools that students will use to promote their own learning. Teachers encourage students to incorporate new knowledge with existing knowledge. They focus on helping students focus on success and creating a positive self-concept. Assessment is performance based.

Constructivism

Constructivism is based on the premise that each learner has a unique background and set of needs. It recognizes students as complex and multidimensional. In a constructivist classroom, teachers encourage students to make their own connections to the learning, and responsibility for learning increasingly lies with the student. In other words, students must be actively involved with the learning process. With this theory, there is an additional focus on social interaction: students learn with and through others.

In constructivism, teachers help students create mental models and teach and encourage them to regulate themselves. There are numerous strategies that are utilized with this theory: reciprocal questioning (students work together to ask and answer questions), jigsaw activities (students become an expert on one aspect of a topic and then teach others), and structured controversies (students work together to research a controversial topic). One type of constructivist assessment is allowing students to demonstrate to the teacher what they have learned. The assessment is appropriate if it convinces the teacher that students know the material.

Experientialism

Experientialism focuses on learning by doing. In this learning theory, students are actively engaged in the learning process and they learn from that experience. Learning happens when students engage. This theory states that learning is a holistic approach influenced by a variety of factors including cognitive processes, emotions, and the environment. Experiential theory requires students to master skills and problem-solve. Students must actively engage in the activity and then reflect on all aspects of the experience. Teachers create or seek opportunities to alter the learning environment so that students can learn by doing.

Contextual

Contextual learning theory is based on the premise that students need to understand concepts and make connections to previous learning, to other concepts, and to real world situations. Teachers must both teach concepts and assist students to make connections. Contextual learning is complex. According to this theory, learning occurs when students learn and process information in a manner that makes sense to them. They retain the information when and because they connect the information to their previous learning and to other concepts they have learned.

Teachers understand that learning can occur in multiple environments and create multiple experiences that include using the classroom, labs, or real world environments. Teachers also focus on creating opportunities for students to connect abstract concepts and ideas with practical and real world applications.

> True teaching, then, is not that which gives knowledge, but that which stimulates pupils to gain it.
>
> Milton Gregory

Regardless of approach or learning theory, research-based instructional strategies, which are referenced later, are important. Knight (2013) notes that most learning theories and approaches can be implemented effectively in the right context, and the use of research-based (high yield) strategies needs to be considered.

Three

Differentiation, Learning Styles, and Thinking Taxonomy

Much has been written about differentiation of instruction and learning styles. While there is some disagreement about the importance of both, instructional and learning leaders need to be aware of the major issues connected to both concepts.

While the Hattie (2011) research does not indicate that differentiation has as large an impact on student learning as other strategies, it is still an important instructional tool having a connection to motivation, retention, and transfer of knowledge. Tomlinson (2010) is an authority on the topic, and her work is valuable for teachers and principals.

While there are numerous ways to differentiate instruction, two major ways include differentiation based around the curriculum and differentiation based around the student. Differentiation around the curriculum allows teachers to differentiate based on content, process, or product, each briefly described below.

- Content Differentiation: Includes having some students working on one topic while others pursue other topics. For example, one group of students can study the causes of World War II, another the political leaders of countries involved, another the technology of the war including weapons, and still another the results of the war.
- Process Differentiation: Some students conduct research on a topic while others are using a text and still others are watching a video.
- Product Differentiation: Students produce different products based on the learning, e.g., writing a paper, creating a game, writing a blog, creating a podcast.

As opposed to differentiation based on curriculum, differentiation around the student allows teachers to make instructional adaptations based on a student's readiness, interest, and learning profile as described below.

- Differentiation based on student readiness: Allows teachers to create leveled objectives based on the content. Redding (2006) refers to

three levels of objectives: prerequisite for students not on grade level, target for those on grade level, and enhanced for those above grade level. Instruction is adapted to meet the needs of the students at each of the levels.
- Instruction differentiated around interest: Gives students an option to explore a topic of special interest. Students will work on different assignments and different topics.
- Differentiation based on learning profile and individual needs and preferences: Some students may be involved in oral instruction while others may be engaged with visual, tactual, or kinesthetic activities to maximize learning.

Dunn's (1993) research identifies twenty-one learning styles that have an impact on student achievement; however, the effect size for each of the twenty-one differs. Dunn organizes the twenty-one styles into five strands: environmental (sound, light, temperature, design); emotional (motivation, persistence, responsibility, structure); sociological (self, pair, team, adult, varied); physical (perceptual, intake, time, mobility); and psychological (global/analytic, left/right hemisphere, impulsive/reflective).

Learning styles research is based on two theories, cognitive style theory and brain lateralization theory. Cognitive style theory revolves around the idea that individuals process information differently which could be the result of either inherent or learned traits. Brain lateralization theory is based on the concept that the two hemispheres of the human brain have different functions.

It is very difficult, and probably not necessary, to focus on all of the identified learning styles. Six styles are worthy of consideration and will be addressed individually. Before this discussion, however, it is important to note that attempting to teach students based solely on the favored learning styles may be counterproductive as students will be expected over their educational careers to engage and learn through a variety of learning styles.

This does not mean that teachers should ignore learning styles, rather, it means teachers should plan and provide instruction utilizing the six learning styles that impact the greatest number of students. Dunn (1993) notes that the six are auditory, visual, tactual, kinesthetic, global, and analytic.

Auditory learners prefer to hear or read information and enjoy listening, lectures, and class discussions. Visual learners, on the other hand, prefer pictures, diagrams, and visual representations, responding to color, images, and graphs. Tactual learners are those students who prefer hands-on experiences that include manipulatives while kinesthetic learners like physical movement, preferring to be actively participating.

Global learners are those who learn from whole to part, needing to see the big picture before examining the component parts. In contrast, analytic learners prefer to learn part to whole, seeing how the components create the big picture. Although there are skeptics who put little faith in learning styles, almost everyone agrees that students learn differently; thus, it makes intuitive sense to utilize a variety of styles when working with students.

There are many ways to examine issues related to critical thinking; however, Bloom (1956) provides an excellent foundation for examining thinking with his taxonomy, and it is his cognitive taxonomy that is referenced here. Many educators consider the first two levels of Bloom (knowledge and comprehension) as lower levels of thinking and the remaining four levels as higher order thinking.

With this in mind, it is important to remember that Bloom's taxonomy is contextual and that the lower level skills (knowledge and comprehension) provide the foundation for higher levels of thinking and so must not be dismissed. Knowledge is the lowest level of Bloom and is simply the ability to recall information. Thinking at this level requires students to define, describe, list, and recognize.

The second level is comprehension which is the ability to state a concept using one's own words. At this level, students comprehend, summarize, rewrite, and paraphrase. Moving up the cognitive ladder, application is the ability to use a concept in a new situation, requiring students to compute, predict, produce, and solve.

Next, analysis demands breaking material down into its component parts, including the ability to illustrate, deconstruct, diagram, and separate. Still higher on Bloom's cognitive ladder, synthesis requires students to take component parts and create something new by combining, compiling, rearranging, and reorganizing. The final level is evaluation. At this level, students make judgments about something and must interpret, justify, defend, and draw conclusions.

The importance of focusing on the taxonomy of cognitive thinking is hard to overemphasize. After all, critical thinking skills are connected to both college and career readiness, and the bottom line is that all students need to think critically. Thus, it is imperative that teachers create questions and develop activities intended to encourage and expect students to perform at higher levels of thinking. Students must expand knowledge and comprehension to higher levels. This does not happen randomly. It must be an intentional process, and teachers must continuously challenge their students to move up the cognitive ladder.

Chapter Three

> We shall require a substantially new manner of thinking if mankind is to survive.
>
> Albert Einstein

Four

The Lesson Line

Madeline Hunter introduced the lesson line as a way to focus on the elements of effective teaching. The lesson line is not labeled in the visual model located earlier in the introduction. It is simply referenced as a line which stretches from the teacher to the objective. Hunter placed those elements she considered important on the line: anticipatory set, objective, method of delivery, activity, practice, retention, reinforcement, transfer, checking for understanding, monitoring and adjusting, and closure.

Hunter's work is the conceptual foundation for the lesson line and what is below the lesson line in this model. Many of the elements of her lesson line are referenced as are additional elements that promote and encourage student learning.

LESSON FRAME

The lesson frame, based on the work of Cain and Laird (2011), is connected to what Madeline Hunter referred to as the anticipatory set. Cain and Laird (2011), however, expand her concept by noting that the teacher's lesson frame should include thought about both the beginning and the end of the lesson. In other words, teachers should know and communicate to students what they are going to learn as well as communicate how students will demonstrate the learning at the end of the period. They argue that the lesson frame must be "a deliberate act" by the teacher. They further note that both the beginning and ending should be written "in concrete, student friendly language" (p. 26).

OBJECTIVE

The objective is the intended learning for the day. It should be SMART: specific, measurable, attainable, relevant, and trackable. It should be standards based and should be at the correct instructional level and the correct level of difficulty. At the end of the day, teachers should be able to determine whether or not students met the objective.

METHOD OF DELIVERY

Method of delivery is exactly what it sounds like. How is the teacher going to present the material to the class? What is the most effective way to deliver the content? It could be lecture, discussion, readings, research, labs, role play, simulations, games, videos, oral recordings, or any number of other options. The key is that the teacher, based on available resources, chooses the best method to deliver the content.

ACTIVITY

Activity refers to how students practice using the material that has been presented. This could be a lab, conducting research, class discussions, guided practice, independent practice, or a variety of other strategies. What is important is that the teacher gives the students an opportunity to interact and engage with the new material.

THOUGHTFUL EXTENSION

As previously noted under the Lesson Frame section, Cain and Laird (2011) emphasize that teachers should know and communicate to students what they are going to learn as well as communicate how students will demonstrate the learning at the end of the period. Both elements are communicated at the beginning of the lesson. While this is powerful, teachers do not want to encourage the idea that learning is over once the lesson is finished. Rather, teachers want to promote learning even after the lesson is over. Training conducted through the National Institute of School Leadership references the term *thoughtful extension*: What is the best way to leave students with the desire to learn more about the content? What will cultivate curiosity and inquiry for future learning? How can a love of learning be generalized? The beauty of learning is that it does not matter where it happens. Teachers who cultivate that love for learning will have students who are eager to learn no matter where they are.

> Curiosity is, in great and generous minds, the first passion and the last.
>
> Samuel Johnson

Five

Research-based Instructional Strategies

Research-based instructional strategies are those teaching strategies that promote student learning. In some of the literature, they are referred to as high-yield strategies. By either definition, there is a body of research which says that these strategies increase the probability that students will learn, absorb, and retain more. Not all research-based instructional strategies are included in the model; in fact, only a few are noted. Nonetheless, administrators need to be familiar with as many strategies as possible so that they can suggest strategies when teachers are struggling and students are not learning.

The key is helping teachers focus on more than one strategy and assisting them in becoming conversant and comfortable using a variety of strategies. It may be thought of as adding tools to a toolbox so that the right tool can be used to address a specific problem or need. One strategy for principals is to have teachers study a research-based (high yield) strategy, try it with their students, and then report the results to the rest of the faculty or members of their professional learning communities (PLCs).

SIMILARITIES AND DIFFERENCES

One of Marzano's (2001) instructional strategies, similarities and differences, encourages students to look for things that are alike and things that are different. Using this strategy, teachers present examples and then encourage students to discuss and/or dig deeper into the content. Students may be given the task to find the similarities and differences on their own. For example, students may use a Venn diagram or a chart to note how things are similar or different. This strategy can be as simple or as complex as the teacher needs to address a particular skill, concept, or content topic.

SUMMARIZING AND NOTE TAKING

Using another Marzano strategy, summarizing and note taking, teachers ask students to summarize what they have learned and put the information into their own words. Because verbatim note taking is often counterproductive, teachers using this strategy must give students time to reflect, process, and absorb the material. One way for teachers to do this is to allow students time to reflect and process followed by an opportunity to write notes in their notebooks or journals. This is an excellent review of the material and also promotes retention of information.

HOMEWORK AND PRACTICE

There is much controversy over homework, but Marzano's research is clear: homework and practice matter. Homework gives students opportunities to practice skills or extend their knowledge outside the classroom. To be effective, homework should be practice of a recently taught concept/skill or connected to future learning. In addition, Marzano states that teachers should provide feedback on homework. Varying homework assignments is also important; in fact, Dunn states that students should occasionally be given the opportunity to develop their own homework assignments, creating or doing something that demonstrates they know the material or can apply the skill.

The amount of homework should vary by grade level, and students, not parents, should do the work. After all, the purpose of homework is for teachers to determine if students know the material, not to see if parents know it. Many school divisions have school board policies related to homework, and administrators need to ensure that teachers understand and follow these policies.

NONLINGUISTIC REPRESENTATION

Students learn through both linguistic and nonlinguistic modes. Many teachers, however, focus on linguistic instruction with readings and lectures as their primary ways to deliver instruction. Though these delivery methods seem to be the norm, the fact is that students also learn effectively in nonlinguistic ways. They learn through creating visual images, participating in hands-on experiences, and moving.

Thus, nonlinguistic teaching strategies include the use of concept maps, role playing, and simulations. Many of the strategies for visual, tactual, and kinesthetic learners are also nonlinguistic. Teachers may have students develop models, draw, or create mental images. Giving students an opportunity to verbalize their models and drawings also helps them identify their thinking.

GENERATING AND TESTING HYPOTHESES

Generating and testing hypotheses can occur in every discipline: What will happen if . . . ? This strategy encourages students to make decisions, investigate, experiment, create, and problem solve. To implement this strategy, teachers need simply to ask students to develop a hypothesis and then test it to see if it is true.

CUES, QUESTIONS, ADVANCE ORGANIZERS

This strategy involves exposing students to information before they learn it. Teachers ask questions and give cues to students related to previous learning. When students recall previous information, teachers help them connect the new learning to what they already know as well as to previously learned concepts. This is important in all disciplines but is especially important in math and science. One of the most overlooked elements of math and science instruction is connecting concepts and helping students see connections and relationships.

Advance organizers give students strategies around which to organize and think about content, helping them to link what they already know to what they are going to learn. Examples include providing new information in a story format, having students skim a chapter or reading assignments to figure out what the new material is about, or directly telling students how the material is connected to previous learning.

INTERACTIVE NOTEBOOK

Interactive notebook is a strategy that encourages students to be independent writers and thinkers. It encourages note taking and at the same time creates a structure for learning, an important process for some students. Students process new learning which may come from class, readings, videos, research, or outside assignments by first summarizing and writing about what they learned and then illustrating their learning through graphic organizers, charts, webs, foldables, in fact, anything that helps students remember the information. Students go back to their notebooks to study and complete connected assignments.

JIGSAW

A jigsaw teaching strategy is a cooperative learning strategy during which students learn with and through others. Students are divided into teams or groups with each member of a team assigned a section of the assignment or research topic. For example, one student may be assigned to look at the causes of the Revolutionary War while another student studies military strategies used by both sides, another student researches military leaders on each side, and yet another student studies the results of the war.

Students must research and learn as much as possible about their assigned section and are expected to become "experts" on their assigned content. Once students have gathered information on their individual sections, they meet with students from other classroom groups who researched the same section. They share their information and learn from each other. They then take what they learn and prepare a presentation for their original group. As a result of each team member's becoming an expert on one section of content, all members of the team learn from each other.

GRAPHIC ORGANIZERS

A graphic organizer is a form of an advance organizer but includes visual representation. While advance organizers can be narrative, graphic organizers include charts, tables, pictograms, and concept webs or maps. The purpose is to figure out what students already know and use it to connect to new material.

WORD WALLS

Words walls, if used correctly, can be powerful strategies in any discipline. Teachers place vocabulary and key terms on the wall. It is important that word walls be changed on a regular basis and that they contain a limited number of words. If there are too many words or the teachers try to place all important words on the wall, it becomes difficult to use the word wall effectively. Teachers use the word wall by referring to the vocabulary/terms often, modeling their use, using the terms during instruction, and including them on tests. Students use the terms during class discussions and in their writing.

MANIPULATIVES

It is well known that the National Council of Teachers of Mathematics (NCTM) promotes the use of manipulatives at all grade levels, but they are useful in other disciplines as well. They help students understand abstract concepts and assist them to think about content in a different way. Manipulatives help students verbalize concepts, problems, and solutions.

The use of manipulatives is directly connected to experiential learning theory and tactual and kinesthetic learning styles. They are also useful in helping students move through Bloom's cognitive thinking taxonomy.

INSIDE/OUTSIDE CIRCLE

As with most of the research-based strategies, inside/outside circle is both a teaching strategy and a formative assessment. Students are divided into two groups with one group (A) forming an outside circle facing the center of the room. The second group (B) forms an inner circle, facing students in the outer circle. Each student is now paired with another student. First, partner A in each pairing shares information with partner B about what the teacher has assigned. Sharing may be summaries of a unit, a reading, a theory, or a document. At the end of the defined time, partner B adds what he knows to the topic. Students then rotate one, two, or three people and re-engage in the same conversation.

METACOGNITION

Metacognition helps students become aware of their own thinking. The process encourages students to develop learning goals, self-monitor progress toward the goals, self-predict, paraphrase, question, and adjust. It is based on a growth mindset that believes intelligence is not static but rather a constantly evolving state. As part of metacognition, teachers must teach students how to plan and set learning goals. They must also help students learn how to monitor their learning and how to adjust their learning when their goals are not being met.

Six

Practice and Retention

Practice is important in the learning process because if done correctly, it helps students absorb and retain new learning. There is an old saying that "practice makes perfect," but this is not true. Practice makes permanent, but only perfect practice makes perfect. If students practice incorrectly, they will learn, but what they learn will be the wrong thing. Teachers then have to go back to undo previous learning before students can absorb and retain new learning. This is what Madeline Hunter calls negative transfer of learning: previous learning that interferes with new learning.

While it is important for students to practice, teachers need to match the practice with intended learning outcomes. Several forms of practice are available to teachers, each with its own purpose. Four forms of practice—guided, independent, mass, and distributed—are discussed below.

THE FOUR FORMS OF PRACTICE

Guided Practice

Guided practice is exactly what it sounds like. While students practice, teachers move around their classroom making sure students practice correctly. This form of practice is often effective when introducing new learning. Toward the end of the learning, teachers use guided practice to check, correct, or redirect students' learning.

Independent Practice

While independent practice can exist in a variety of formats, it is most often thought of as homework. Teachers assign work for students to complete outside of class.

Mass Practice

Mass practice simply means giving students many problems and questions to complete. It is generally most effective with new learning when students need a great deal of repetition to learn. Students must practice with enough problems or questions to become comfortable with the learning, but not so many that they become sloppy in their work. Teachers need to assign enough work for students to concentrate on the material but not so much that students fail to put forth their best effort. Since practice makes permanent, too much practice could lead to problems learning the material.

Distributed Practice

Distributed practice is the form of practice that is most often overlooked. This form of practice means that teachers give students opportunities to continue practicing the skill or using the knowledge after it has been learned and assessed. Big ideas from previous learning continue to be referenced, discussed, and tested, thus reinforcing and promoting long-term memory and retention. Most teachers provide knowledge, teach a skill, provide guided practice, mass practice the content, give independent practice, and finally test the content. They then move to the next topic or concept in the curriculum and do not intentionally focus on previously learned material.

This means that most teachers, three weeks before the state assessment, spend three weeks reviewing what was previously taught, hoping that students will retain it for the state assessment. On the other hand, teachers who have consistently used distributed practice should have students who, having practiced throughout the year, are much better prepared. Being intentional about distributed practice gives teachers an opportunity to help students see connections between content, concepts, and skills. Distributed practice promotes connections.

Some teachers argue they do not have time to reinforce and retest previous learning; however, if practice is distributed and teachers do not need to spend three weeks reviewing for a test, they pick up two to three weeks of additional instructional time before the test.

RETENTION

Retention is a major component of learning. If students do not retain the learning and cannot make connections of previous learning to new learning, what good has it done for them to have "learned" it in the first place? Learning must inform the future. Learning that is retained allows students to use previous information to make connections with new learning and see how concepts and principles are connected. Teachers have to be intentional about creating a learning environment that promotes retention.

Learning involves both the brain and the environment. Unfortunately, it is possible and even common for students to learn something, be able to share it for a short period of time, and then forget it. The goal of learning, however, is to promote long-term memory. Teachers want students to retain the learning so that the brain can locate, identify, and retrieve the information in the future.

In retaining learning, the time between learning the material and using it is critical. The shorter the elapsed time between learning and using, the greater the retention of the learning. Retention is also aided when teachers personalize learning by encouraging student reflection in a variety of ways (discussion, writing, applying, evaluating).

Furthermore, to increase retention, teachers must be intentional about using multiple modes of instructional delivery. Lecture, reading, audiovisual, and demonstrating (modeling) are passive—but often effective—strategies if the teacher is intentional about how they are used. Discussions, active verbal and written reflection, practice, and having students teach something to others are active strategies, also effective when the teacher uses them in the right situation.

Retention is also connected to the degree of original learning. Because how well students learned previous material is important to retention, teachers must engage in vertical conversations about curriculum, instruction, and assessment (CIA). For example, every teacher should be familiar with the CIA from the previous year and the next year. All need to know how their instruction is influenced by what went on before and what will happen after.

It is important for teachers to have a mindset that they have to teach what students need to know. A superstar teacher never says, "You were supposed to learn that last year." If students do not have the prerequisite knowledge to learn the new skill, teachers have to teach it. For example, a high school geometry teacher should have the knowledge and skill set to teach K–9 math. For retention to happen, teachers must analyze what students need and teach it, even if it should have been taught and learned two years ago.

The final point concerning retention is that material must be relevant to students for retention to occur. Teachers must share with students how the information is relevant to them now and in the future. They should help students reflect on the relevance. Teachers who intentionally make connections between previous and new learning promote relevance for students.

Seven

Reinforcement and Intangibles

REINFORCEMENT

There are three types of reinforcement that are important in the classroom: positive, negative, and extinction. Many classroom management systems and school-wide discipline programs focus on a system of rewards and punishments.

Positive Reinforcement

Positive reinforcement is when teachers reinforce and recognize appropriate behavior or something good the student has done. Its purpose is for students to continue use of the behavior that led to the reinforcement. Rewards and encouragement are considered positive reinforcement. Teachers recognize, reward, and praise when students act consistently with established expectations.

Negative Reinforcement

Negative reinforcement is a type of punishment. When students exhibit inappropriate behavior, teachers often use negative reinforcement, such as an admonishment or consequence, in an attempt to change the behavior.

Extinction

Extinction means ignoring the behavior. The purpose of this strategy is to change behavior but without confronting the student. When teachers believe students are acting inappropriately to get attention, they may choose to ignore the behavior. Teachers are counting on students to change the behavior because they did not get the response expected.

There are a number of intangible, harder to measure characteristics that influence student learning. Among these are eye contact, expression/tone, movement, personalization, motivation, and relationships.

REINFORCEMENT AND MINDSET

When using reinforcement in the classroom, it is important to reinforce the right things. Often educators praise natural ability and intelligence. They praise perfection and speed. Dweck (2006) argues that "speed and perfection are the enemy of difficult learning" (p. 179). Reinforcement should recognize effort and persistence.

Eye Contact

Principals should make eye contact with teachers, and teachers should make eye contact with students. However, whether or not eye contact is returned should not be a deal breaker. Failure to return eye contact may have many reasons, and teachers and administrators should not give meaning to the behavior unless there is clear evidence that failure to make eye contact is intended to be disrespectful. That intent is difficult to prove, so it is best for teachers to model what should occur.

Modeling is also preferable, as opposed to requiring reciprocity, in diverse public schools which may well include students from cultures and subcultures that consider eye contact to be disrespectful. Perhaps the worst thing that can happen is for the teacher to state, "Look me in the eye when I am talking to you," as this backs students in a corner, makes them defensive, and rarely leads to increased learning. Teachers need to be intentional about minimizing problems, not creating them.

Expression/Tone

Teachers need to demonstrate energy in many ways, including through vocal expression and tone of voice. A monotone voice and/or a negative tone of voice generally do not create a classroom environment that promotes learning.

Movement

Teacher movement around the classroom is important even during a lecture or other teacher-directed activities. Proximity to the teacher keeps students on task and brings them back to focusing on what they should be doing if their attention wanders. If teachers do not believe that proximity changes behavior, they should be reminded of what most people do when they are driving and see a police officer. Almost everyone brakes. Proximity matters, and teachers who sit at their desks or stand in one location in the classroom rarely engage their students fully in the learning process.

Personalization

The importance of personalization cannot be overemphasized. Classrooms and schools must embrace a culture of personalization as NASSP's *Breaking Ranks®* initiative emphasizes by its inclusion of personalization as one of its three major concepts. The six elements of the personalization piece of *Breaking Ranks®* are listed below with a brief description.

- Recognition—creating equitable opportunities for students to create their own voices and be acknowledged for who they are
- Acceptance—providing opportunities for students to join a caring community of adults and peers
- Trust—providing opportunities and choices for students to demonstrate trust
- Respect—providing opportunities for students to be responsible and demonstrate responsible behavior
- Purpose—providing opportunities for students to imagine and dream about what they can become and challenging them to get there
- Confirmation—creating high expectations for students' success around high standards

Motivation

Motivation can drive or encourage a student to act. It affects effort and effort affects achievement. It creates energy. Some students are already motivated to achieve when they come to school, but motivation can also come from the school and/or the environment. Both school-wide and classroom efforts to motivate students through extrinsic means (a system of rewards) have their place, but it is intrinsic motivation that is most critical. Teachers should consistently promote intrinsic (internal) motivation, for it is intrinsic motivation that sustains student effort.

RELATIONSHIPS

Some educators argue that the new 3R's are rigor, relevance, and relationships. Many non-educators, including some politicians, argue that schools must be rigorous and focus on content that is relevant for the present and the future. Not many educators oppose that argument, but many educators understand that rigor and relevance are very hard to achieve if teachers do not build relationships with students.

The quality of the relationship between teacher and student is critical to the learning process. Furthermore, relationships are strongly connected to student retention of information and personalization. *Breaking Ranks®* materials state emphatically that students need to be connected to adults they can see themselves becoming.

> *Some argue that the new 3 R's are rigor, relevance, and relationships, but in reality, the new 3 R's are relationships, rigor, and relevance. It all starts with relationships.*
>
> —Roger Jones

There is some excellent work around relationships that is included in the original *Breaking Ranks®* material. The emphasis is around six fundamental relationships that are important to most students and previously noted under personalization. These relationships need to be examined around how they connect to the personal needs of students as well as how classroom or school practices impact these relationships.

Schools are the most logical place to support and build these relationships. All students will, over time, develop the six relationships. They will be recognized, accepted, trusted, respected, given a purpose, and confirmed. Unfortunately, if schools do not do their part in building these relationships, other less positive organizations will. Students often seek gang membership to satisfy the need for relationships.

Schools must examine school and classroom practices to build these relationships and to meet the personal needs of students. Often, school and classroom practices interfere with building relationships. For example, school recognition programs often recognize only select groups of students such as academic scholars and athletes. However, student voices may be projected in community service activities, music, arts, leadership, or any number of other activities.

Each of the relationships is examined in more depth in the following chart.

Another resource for meeting the needs of students is found in the work of the Search Institute. They have identified forty developmental assets which are "common sense, positive experiences and qualities that help influence choices young people make and help them become caring, responsible, successful adults." Their work, based on research and effec-

Table 7.1.

Personal Needs	Relationships	School/Class Practices
Voice Every student needs to have a voice. What are the student's strengths? What is he or she good at?	**Recognition** Being recognized is important to students.	**Equity** Do school and classroom practices allow students to develop their own talents and strengths?
Belonging Every student wants to belong to something.	**Acceptance** Students want to be accepted.	**Community** Do school and classroom practices create opportunities for students to be accepted? If not, students will seek opportunities to be accepted in other endeavors, such as gangs.
Choice Every student benefits from having to make choices.	**Trust** Students want to be trusted.	**Opportunity** Do school and classroom practices allow students to demonstrate they can be trusted?
Freedom Every student benefits from having some freedom that leads to gaining respect from others.	**Respect** Students want to be respected.	**Responsibility** Do school and classroom practices give students opportunities to earn respect?
Imagination Every student needs to be able to imagine what he/she can become.	**Purpose** Students want a sense of purpose in their life.	**Challenge** Do school and classroom practices allow students to explore options that let them imagine the future?
Success Every student wants to be successful in such a way that will confirm their value to others.	**Confirmation** Students want confirmation that they are good and worthy people.	**Expectations** Do school and classroom practices create high expectations for all students so that their success is actually meaningful?

tiveness, is one of the most widely used approaches in developing youth in the country. Information can be found at http://www.search-institute.org/. Developmental assets are provided for four age groups including adolescents (ages 12–18), middle childhood (ages 8–12), grades K–3 (ages 5–9), and early childhood (ages 3–5).

Eight

Student Engagement

Instructional leadership focusing on teacher behaviors that promote student learning must pay diligent attention to teacher behaviors and decisions related to student engagement. Determining whether or not students are engaged with the content is both a subjective and objective experience, and so teachers and administrators should be aware of a variety of issues as they evaluate student engagement. These issues are categorized under three areas of engagement: behavioral, cognitive, and emotional.

ENGAGEMENT

Behavioral Engagement

Although it is generally accepted that teachers must establish expectations or rules for their classrooms, there exists disagreement about the respective value of rules and expectations. Some argue that rules have a negative connotation and that a focus on obeying rules results in a preponderance of negative consequences. Expectations, on the other hand, are often seen as more positive, as helping to create a classroom environment that focuses on what students can become.

While this author is biased toward expectations, it is nonetheless important for teachers to establish structures that promote good classroom management. After all, students must feel safe in both the school and the classroom to be able to learn. It is also important for teachers to be intentional about monitoring students' attention and time on task and about creating some system of accountability that promotes behavioral engagement.

Cognitive Engagement

Numerous factors promote cognitive engagement. Students should have learning goals that challenge and encourage them to meet high expectations. While teachers should use a variety of strategies, it is important for students to be active and engaged with the learning. As previously noted, the less time that elapses between learning and using the new content, the better.

Teachers should also promote, encourage, and recognize students' successes by celebrating both small and large learning gains. Success breeds success. Just as important as experiencing success is the opportunity to be creative. Teachers can increase cognitive engagement by allowing students frequent chances to get their creative juices flowing.

Teachers also promote cognitive engagement in many other ways. They need to probe and provide cues and clues that require students to think about the content. Teachers who are serious about engaging students cognitively do not let them "off the hook," instead, pushing them to think and to take their thinking to another level. These teachers understand the value of wait time and learn to pause so that students have time to think about their responses. Too often, teachers will provide wait time for the students they believe know the answer but do not provide wait time for those who may not. It does not take long for students to figure out teacher expectations and to adjust their cognitive engagement accordingly.

Just as there must be accountability for behavioral engagement, there must also be accountability for cognitive engagement. Teachers must emphasize and students must realize that the responsibility for learning lies with each student. Teachers do everything they can to encourage and promote student engagement, but ultimately, each student must accept responsibility for the learning. Though this is true, teachers must not fall back on the old adage, "I taught it, but they did not learn it." Teachers have a huge responsibility to their students to be a learning leader just as principals have that same responsibility to their teachers.

Teachers also impact cognitive engagement through the questions they ask. Teachers often, without realizing it, set low expectations for some students through the questions they ask. When teachers ask "C" and below students only knowledge and comprehension questions, they are establishing expectations that prevent these students from rising to higher cognitive levels. Some teachers may do this to give students a feeling of success, but it does not take students long to figure out the level of questions being asked and to realize that teachers do not expect them to push and challenge themselves.

When students cannot answer a more difficult question, teachers should not let them "off the hook." Instead, they may implement a strategy such as calling on another student for the answer but then coming back to the original student with the question again. It does not matter if the student learns the material from the teacher or from another student. What matters is that he learns it.

Teachers also need to be intentional about how they group students. Every grouping of students should have a purpose, and teachers should be able to articulate the purpose for the grouping pattern and how it relates to cognitive engagement.

Emotional Engagement

A third element of student engagement is emotional engagement. Students who are emotionally engaged are more vested, interested, and committed to the learning. First, teachers need to reinforce that effort matters and that students must give their best effort in the learning process. Teachers must use language that encourages students to stay with the learning and not give up, to be persistent and to stick with it when the going gets tough. What the teacher says is critical in this endeavor. Statements such as those below should be heard frequently.

- You can do it.
- Do not give up on me.
- Do not give up on yourself.
- Effort matters.
- Persistence matters.
- Nothing worth achieving is achieved easily.
- You control your attitude, your effort, and your commitment.

Students should also be encouraged to take pride in the quality of their work and to think like an artisan, willing to sign their work. They need to be encouraged to delight in their accomplishments. Working hard, making the extra effort, and achieving something challenging should result in students feeling great about what they have done.

Teachers must have a growth mindset and must promote a growth mindset in their students. Dweck (2006) states that teachers generally display one of two types of mindsets. They either believe that learning and intelligence are fixed or that learning and intelligence can be improved with effort, commitment, and great teaching. Superstar teachers have growth mindsets: all teachers should have and display this mindset every day. Administrators must insist on it.

> Perpetual optimism is a force multiplier. The ripple effect of enthusiasm and optimism is awesome. So is the impact of cynicism and pessimism. Those who whine and blame engender those same behaviors among their colleagues. There has to be a gung-ho attitude, which says "we can change things here, we can achieve awesome goals, we can be the best." Spare me the grim litany of the "realist," give me the unrealistic aspirations of the optimist any day.
>
> Colin Powell

Teachers know that student engagement promotes learning and long-term memory. How can teachers influence student engagement? Students become more engaged and remain more engaged when they are successful. Self-efficacy is the belief in one's ability to be successful. It is related to effort, persistence, and commitment. Teachers must create classrooms that promote self-efficacy.

There are two necessary components linked to student engagement: teacher behavior and student behavior. Teacher behavior is the area where both teachers and administrators have placed most of their attention. When teacher behavior becomes the primary focus, it is very easy for the teacher to do all the work. However, students must be actively involved in the lesson.

There is a difference between student activity and student engagement. Just having a hands-on activity is not necessarily real student engagement. Thus the focus must be on teacher behavior that encourages student engagement and student behavior that demonstrates student engagement.

Many educators have researched and written about both teacher behavior and student engagement including DiPaola (2007), Hattie (2011), Hunter (2004), Marzano (2003), and Tomlinson (2010). Listed below are some ideas and strategies that promote student learning. Some are referenced in other sections. Some come from teachers at two high schools in Lynchburg, VA. The lists are provided to give administrators a foundation from which to generate conversations with teachers.

STRATEGIES TO PROMOTE STUDENT LEARNING

Teacher Behaviors that Encourage Student Engagement

- Models clear and high expectations in the classroom.
- Encourages student discussion of daily objectives to make sure students understand.

Student Engagement 37

- Anchors new knowledge through guided practice and modeling of new steps.
- Provides differentiated/tiered/personalized instruction based on student performance.
- Provides learning activities that are sufficiently challenging and, at the same time, within the learner's "performance ability."
- Models metacognitive processing (predicting, paraphrasing, self-questioning, visual representation, changing reading speed).
- Provides ongoing assessment before, during, and after instruction.
- Provides formative/descriptive feedback on the learning process, not just acknowledging the "correct answer."
- Uses probing questions and hints, and scaffolds cues when encouraging all students to think about their answers, not just high achieving students.
- Tells the student what s/he has done correctly and what s/he needs to do to be successful.
- Provides students with examples of what "A" work looks like.
- Provides descriptive feedback.
- Demonstrates interest in and cares about lives of individual students.
- Develops a one-on-one relationship with each student so there is a sense of "relatedness."
- Provides opportunities for learner input into decision making—voice—by involving learners in the design of rubrics that enumerate expectations.
- Provides opportunities for self assessment—formative assessment without a grade.
- Gives options in completing assignments.

Student Behaviors that Demonstrate Student Engagement

- Engages in setting learning goals.
- Engages in making choices.
- Engages in reading.
- Engages in writing.
- Engages in discussing text or other input.
- Engages in problem solving.
- Creates products.
- Engages in peer tutoring, cooperative learning, reciprocal teaching, and other cooperative group structures.
- Engages in relevant, real-world learning experiences.
- Applies meta-cognition strategies which include the following examples: making connections; inferring; generating hypotheses/predicting; asking/generating questions; determining importance/

big ideas; summarizing; visualizing; synthesizing; monitoring and clarifying.
- Creates and uses learning tools including the following: concept maps, advance/graphic organizers; manipulatives; and/or technology.
- Engages in self-assessment of their work, what they learn, and how they learn.
- Engages in asking for and giving specific feedback to peers and to the teacher.
- Talks about ideas with other students.
- Thinks about how information is related to other subjects and to their own lives.
- Thinks critically by asking questions.
- Demonstrates meaningful use of facts and skills.
- Demonstrates what they know before beginning the unit (pre-assessment).
- Takes sides on an issue and explains a point of view.
- Solves difficult problems before end of unit.
- Explores topics that excite/interest them.
- Determines how they demonstrate their learning (choices).

Additional strategies that support student learning include the following:

- Students have reflection time for every fifteen minutes of lecture. Students interact with the material and/or each other in order to retain the information and become engaged in the learning.
- Students provide responses that snowball (or complete a 1-2-4-8 activity). Pose a question for discussion, and students think about the answer. The student joins with another student and shares the answer. Then the two students join with two other students and share answers. This group of four can join with another group to have a group of eight.
- Students use clickers to answer teacher questions.
- Students create web maps, concept maps, thinking maps which demonstrate that they can connect the learning.
- Students create their own rubrics for scoring an assignment.
- Students create their own test around new content.
- Students determine their own way to demonstrate to the teacher that they learned the material.
- Students maintain journals/notebooks.
- Create pictures to summarize information.
- Use "Think/Pair/Share." Pose a question or present a dilemma which should elicit discussion, and each student initially answers it

individually. Students then share their thoughts/ideas with another student (or two or three). Each group of students chooses the best response or a new collective response they have created in their group to share with the class. This way, every student has participated in some way.
- Provide interaction and mingle opportunities through working in pairs, group work, and interviews.
- Analyze standards in the content. Identify vocabulary words and concepts. Create bulletin boards and word walls. Use the vocabulary while teaching and have students use the vocabulary in discussion, assignments, and projects. Use the vocabulary on assessments.
- Give students opportunities to demonstrate their knowledge by creating posters, projects, presentations, talks, and/or recitals.
- Teaching what you have learned to someone else or in front of the class enhances retention. Have students put what they have learned into their own words. Create opportunities for them to share what they have learned through pairing students for discussion, writing a blog post, or creating a podcast.
- Create opportunities for students to use the Smart Board to share information or solve problems.
- Have students quiz each other.
- Use "Random Bucket" strategy where student's names are drawn out of a bucket to answer/respond to questions.
- Use "I'm Determined Strategies." Students focus on being persistent and determined.
- Students write out questions from the reading or class assignments they feel are important and should be on the test. Select questions from each student to include on the quiz.
- Utilize peer questions strategy. Peer questions are student made multiple choice questions. Students create these questions in multiple choice format, and they will trade their questions with other members of the class. Use this activity as a review.
- Utilize Smart Exchange (http://exchange.smarttech.com/) which provides a variety of discipline-related experiences/activities for the Smart Board.
- The Quizlet website (http://quizlet.com/) can be used to generate, use, or download flashcards. This site is great for vocabulary and terms review. If the teacher has an account, s/he can generate her/his own, but if not, there are many sets of flashcards created by others.
- Create Long Posters—perhaps six to eight feet long where all students must put their mark as a review of the assignment or chapter. They use pictures, graphs, graphics, questions, and statements to

demonstrate their section of the content. When completed, the entire chapter is spelled out for the class on a poster chart. This can be used to revisit the information at a later date (distributed practice).
- Engage students in meaningful conversations.

Nine

Formative Assessment

Often, schools, administrators, teachers, and students are evaluated based on summative assessments that generally take the form of state or common core tests, end-of-course tests, or statewide assessments. But, it is not the summative assessments that lead to learning; it is the teacher's ability to use formative assessment effectively that is essential to learning leadership. It is through formative assessment that teachers understand if students have learned the material. Thus, formative assessment must be regular, ongoing, and include a variety of strategies to check for understanding in an effective manner.

In fact, the overall purpose of formative assessment is to gauge what students know to determine if instructional adjustments need to be made. It is the data from formative assessments that allow teachers to monitor and adjust teaching and learning. If students are not learning the content, it is useless to continue to use the same strategies and expect different results.

> *Insanity is doing the same thing over and over and expecting different results.*
>
> —Albert Einstein

Instructional and learning leadership are not about "gotcha teaching." Instead, they are about student learning, about making adjustments so that the end result is improved student achievement. Formative assessment is critical to accomplishing this end, and a variety of strategies may be used, several of which are highlighted below.

FORMATIVE ASSESSMENT STRATEGIES

Pre/post-tests are one effective strategy. Teachers test students on what they know before instruction and use pre-test results to plan instruction and differentiate. Following the unit, students take a post-test to determine if they have learned the material.

Hattie (2011) noted that one of the strategies having the greatest effect on student learning is feedback. To be most effective, feedback must let students know what they are doing well, what is wrong with what they are doing, and what specifically they must do to improve. Teachers generally do a good job of letting students know what they do well and what errors they make; however, they often omit the most important piece: letting students know precisely what they need to do to get better.

Numerous "checking" strategies can provide excellent formative data for teachers. For example, teachers can often find out what students know and do not know by checking notebooks and journals. They can also find out if students are on track by checking homework, by reading rough drafts, or by monitoring in-process assignments.

Think/Pair/Share is another strategy to use in the classroom to have students reflect on their learning and for teachers to "listen" and hear what students understand or do not understand. Teachers have students think about a problem, pair off with other students, and then share information about the topic. As students share, teachers monitor the conversations and pinpoint problem areas that need additional instruction.

In technology driven classrooms, the use of a clicker or response system allows students to use letters (A, B, C, D) or numbers to respond to teacher-generated questions. The advantage of this strategy is that every student participates and feedback for the teacher is instantaneous.

Using an exit ticket is a quick way to assess learning at the end of class. Teachers have students take out a piece of paper and write two or three sentences about the day's learning or a concept or idea that was taught. The papers are collected as students exit the classroom, and teachers review them quickly and place them in three piles: those who got it, those who are close, and those who did not get it.

A variation is to have students write a three-minute paper focusing around what, so what, now what. What did you learn? What does it mean? How can you use the information? A simpler second variation is the one-sentence summary. Teachers ask students to state in one sentence the big idea they took from the day's lesson.

While mind/concept/web maps (similar ideas arranged around an identified topic) can be a teacher tool to help students organize learning or assist teachers themselves in presenting information, they may also be used as a tool for teachers to assess student learning. Teachers provide students with a mind/concept/web map, and students use the map to communicate what they have learned. Many varieties of maps are available; a simple Google search of mind, concept, or web maps will provide numerous examples.

Of course, teachers can determine if students know the material the "old fashioned" way, by giving them a quiz or a test to determine learning. The key is how the teacher uses the test or quiz. Quizzes and tests that inform the teaching process, that provide specifics to the teachers to use in instruction, are valuable.

The use of rubrics is still another way to assess student learning. Rubrics are scoring guidelines that provide consistency and let students know what is expected of them. They also allow teachers to measure student learning more objectively and to identify where students are having major problems so that instruction can be adjusted accordingly.

Finally, the use of reflection is a valuable formative assessment strategy. While it can be integrated with some of the above strategies, the purpose of reflection is to have students connect to the content. One strategy is to frame reflection, as previously referenced, around three elements—what, so what, now what. What did you learn? What does it mean? How can you use the information?

The strategies noted above and many others are effective in helping teachers assess whether or not students know the content. This is the easy part. The critical part of teaching is what teachers do once they know that students have learned or not learned the material. This is where the master teachers make a difference by adjusting their instruction to make sure students know the material. Following are several types of adjustments that teachers can make.

FORMATIVE ASSESSMENT EVIDENCE OF USE

Adjusting instruction means adapting teaching to student needs, that is, changing strategies and activities or differentiating as necessary. Frequently, teachers may use their knowledge of learning styles to change the way material is delivered. What is critical is that teachers do not let students fail when they know students do not get it.

Using data from formative assessments, teachers may re-teach the material to a group of students while providing enrichment activities (horizontal learning) to others. Teachers may also decide to accelerate learning for some students, allowing them to move vertically to new material.

Teachers may also provide verbal and written feedback based on formative assessments to help students who have not learned the material. If the feedback is specific and lets students know exactly what they need to do to get better, it will impact student learning if the student acts on it.

Most schools have learning safety nets that provide interventions for students. Therefore, another effective use of formative assessment is referring the student for intervention. If schools are using a response to intervention (RTI), there will be tier two and tier three interventions available.

Still another effective adjustment in response to formative assessment may be re-grouping. If several students are having the same problem, putting them together in a group and teaching the content in a different way may be helpful.

Teachers need to model how student work can be improved. Specific feedback noting what the student needs to do to meet the standard is absolutely essential. Students should not have to guess what the teacher is looking for. Finally, the student must act on the feedback. No matter how specific the feedback, if students do not act on the feedback, learning will not occur. Students must accept responsibility for their own learning. Learning is a two-way street between the teacher and the student. Both have responsibility for that learning.

Ten

The Essential Twelve

Leading a school in which student learning is the top priority is a challenging process. Knowledge of all the components around this model is important, but all schools should have a set of non-negotiables in which everyone believes and to which everyone adheres. This belief structure should permeate a school and become central to its culture. Every school must develop these non-negotiables around its own needs because each school is different with its own DNA. Despite differences in schools, however, the following twelve essential beliefs provide a strong foundation for a discussion of non-negotiables in every school.

TWELVE ESSENTIAL BELIEFS

1. Educators Must be Instructional and Learning Leaders

Everyone in the school must focus on instructional and learning leadership and look for effective teacher behaviors that promote student learning. Likewise, all school personnel should be willing to try new ideas, challenge themselves, and engage in conversations that focus on instruction. Professional learning communities (PLCs) should be venues for many of those conversations as should faculty meetings.

The culture of the school must also embrace conversations about learning, not just about teaching. Learning and teaching after all go hand in hand. Teachers and administrators must have conversations about how teachers know that learning is taking place. They need to ask and answer the question, "What is the evidence that the teaching strategies being utilized are making a difference in student learning?"

2. Effort and Persistence Lead to Increased Learning

The importance of effort and persistence cannot be overemphasized. There are no entitlements to learning. Students have a responsibility to learn, to accept accountability for their own learning. This belief must be promoted and reinforced by teachers, administrators, and parents. Effort and persistence relate to the attitudes and mindsets of both teachers and students. Teachers must understand and promote the connection between effort and achievement.

Though students are indeed responsible for their own learning, this belief must not be used by teachers to justify a student's lack of progress. "I taught it, but they didn't learn it" is an inappropriate response. Learning is about principals creating a culture of achievement, teachers constantly looking for ways to deliver instruction more effectively and creating ways to measure student learning gains, and students making an effort and taking pride in the work they do. It is also about parents supporting the school and their child and creating a home culture in which learning is important.

Creating a home culture of learning does not depend on the educational level of the parents or on the language spoken in the home; instead, it depends on parents letting their children know that learning is valued in the home and that they, the children, are expected to give their best effort. Students have to be persistent even when they do not learn something the first time.

Unfortunately, students do not always realize the importance of effort and must learn both that they can change their beliefs and that effort matters. It is up to administrators, teachers, staff, and parents to emphasize and encourage a focus on effort.

> Unless we can keep students believing that the goal is within reach, they'll stop trying . . . [and] when the feedback suggests to me that I'm not making it, leading me to an inference that I'm incapable of making it, then I give up in hopelessness and I stop trying. . . . I've got to get them (students) to somehow believe that effort is of value, that there is some relationship between effort and their level of success. If I can't get them to believe that, then I can't help them.
>
> Richard Stiggins as quoted by Jim Knight (2013) in *High-Impact Teaching: A Framework for Great Teaching*, p. 57.

3. *Quality Teaching Matters*

Not only is it common sense, but there is significant research noting that the important variable in the classroom is the quality of the teacher.

Without a doubt, the teacher makes a difference in student learning, but that difference can be either positive or negative. The focus in schools should not be that teaching matters; rather, it should be that quality teaching matters.

Fortunately, there are superstar teachers in most buildings, but the key to school improvement and increased student learning is helping average teachers become more like superstars. This happens when there is an expectation in the building that great teaching matters. It happens when administrators create a culture around student learning, when conversations in buildings focus on ways to help students learn. It happens when there is an intentional effort to promote, encourage, recognize, and celebrate great teaching.

4. Learning Takes Time but Must Lead to College and Career Ready Graduates

Students learn at different rates. Because all students are not going to understand, apply, and analyze the material at the same time, teachers must make adjustments and accommodations for variances in learning. However, even with these differences among students and their rate of learning, it is critical that when they graduate, they are ready for college or career. The skills needed for the twenty-first century are in many ways very different from those of the twentieth century. As Pink (2006) notes, the left brain, sequential, logical, right answer focus is still important. In other words, students in the twenty-first century still need to know and understand content.

At the same time, the right brain skills are also important: the ability to see the big picture, be creative, work with and through others, and make conceptual connections. This expanded knowledge and skill set, clearly articulated by the Partnership for 21st Century Skills (at http://www.p21.org/), includes the following: alignment of curriculum, instruction, and assessment; core subjects; critical thinking; problem solving; collaboration; creativity; innovation; life and career skills; and technology skills.

Although each state defines and measures college and career ready in different ways, each state does indeed define and measure it. It is incumbent on educators to know their state's definition and to understand how they are moving their students to meet this standard.

5. High Expectations Promote Learning

Low expectations have no place in public schools. Students must be taught a rigorous curriculum, and educators must believe that their students can meet higher expectations. Most students will perform at the level expected, so the key is setting high expectations and expecting students to achieve them. That means educators have to be cheerleaders, motivators, encouragers, coaches, and whatever else it takes.

In the interconnected world of teaching and learning, it is important for educators to realize that the types of thinking expected of students have much to do with the level of expectations. Educators must be *intentional* every day about creating high expectations because these expectations cannot exist in the abstract. High expectations must be real and meaningful for students. Educators must constantly keep the concept of high expectations in front of their students.

6. Vision, Non-negotiables, and Intentionality Create a Trifecta for Success

In a study of Virginia schools, Jones and Wheeler (2011) found that sixteen common themes existed in schools that had been identified by the Virginia Department of Education as schools having made significant progress in student achievement over a period of years. Three of the themes—vision, non-negotiables, and intentionality—form a trifecta for school success; every school focused or refocused on vision. Some schools needed to create a new vision, and some just needed to live their vision. Regardless, all schools realized that vision was the starting point for everything else.

Vision alone, however, cannot get the job done. Every school needs to have a set of non-negotiables, a set of standards and expectations that everyone believes in, adheres to, and promotes. The "essential twelve," outlined in this document, provide a good start for determining the non-negotiables in a school.

While the Essential Twelve provide a start, it is important that all educators in a school be involved in conversations about the non-negotiables. They should not be handed down from on high but developed from the ground up. Finally, all educators must focus on what is important; what is important gets done, and educators always find time to do what is important. If everything is important, then nothing is important. Being intentional about what is important is a crucial step to improving student learning.

7. Growth Mindsets Are a Foundation for Increased Student Learning

Dweck (2006) has done significant work around mindsets by studying teachers who have fixed mindsets and those who have growth mindsets. A fixed mindset is a belief that intelligence is fixed and cannot be increased, that is a student's level of achievement will plateau and not show much growth above an expected level over the years. A growth mindset is exactly the opposite.

This mindset believes that intelligence is not static, that it grows and expands as students are challenged, motivated, and encouraged to learn. An educator's mindset informs practice. Dweck's research is very clear: teachers who have a growth mindset have students who achieve at a higher level.

8. Motivation Matters, Intrinsic Motivation Matters More

Most forms of motivation matter. Some schools and teachers establish extrinsic or external reward systems that reward individual students, a class of students, and even schools. If this form of motivation works, it makes sense to continue. While these external rewards might reap benefits, Pink's (2010) work suggests that intrinsic motivation matters more. When students work hard and achieve because of a personal desire to achieve and learn, a foundation for life-long learning is created.

Pink states that autonomy, mastery, and purpose motivate most people when working in high cognitive areas. People want to work independently and be responsible for their own work. They want to get better at what they do, and they want to connect to something that is bigger than themselves. So, in the motivation of both faculty and students, considerable thought should be given to how autonomy, mastery, and purpose can be integrated more formally into motivation systems.

9. Tight Alignment of Curriculum, Instruction,
and Assessment Makes a Difference

The tight alignment of curriculum, instruction, and assessment is a critical component of successful schools. When schools are not successful, the reason is often a lack of tight alignment. School administrators and teachers often state and may believe that the curriculum is aligned but, upon a close analysis, they find it is not. For example, Jones and Wheeler (2011) found that the schools in their study originally believed they had close alignment. However, as schools undertook a closer look at alignment, they realized that what was written, taught, and tested were not congruent. At that point, schools developed a more effective alignment and significant improvement began.

In a school with tight alignment, the curriculum must address state standards, instruction must be based on the curriculum, and assessments must demonstrate student proficiency of the standards. There are many ways to encourage and promote such an alignment including the use of curriculum maps, frameworks, and pacing guides. All of these are referenced in the planning phase of this document.

Educators must be very intentional about this topic. Careful consideration should be given to checking the level of difficulty of questions, activities, assignments, and tests to ensure that all match the rigor of the standard. If the level of rigor of classroom instruction and teacher-developed tests do not match the rigor of the assessment, student achievement will suffer.

Principals need to remind teachers constantly of the importance of tight alignment. They need to examine lesson plans, observe instruction, talk with teachers about classroom decisions, and review teacher-developed assessments. In addition, PLCs should include a constant monitoring of where teachers are in teaching the standards, a discussion of teaching strategies that are working, and an agreement that assessments measure the standards, all of which will help ensure better alignment.

10. Feedback Must Stimulate Action

Feedback is critically important, and it must be specific. Writing "good work" on a paper or adding a smiley face is not feedback because these do not sufficiently inform students about what they have done well and what they need to do to get better. Effective feedback gives students enough information to stimulate them to take action. Students must act on the feedback for it to be effective.

Feedback to students should encourage self-assessment and should be viewed as a strategy to motivate students to higher levels of achievement. Students must understand the feedback and must be able to act on the feedback.

11. Every Child, by Need, Every Day

Earlier reference was made to the importance of vision. Vision is the future, but mission is the charge! Every child, by need, every day must be the charge of every teacher and every principal. This should be the mission that drives the school every single day.

This belief should be a part of every set of non-negotiables within a school. Students need to be connected to an adult they can see themselves becoming. Therefore, educators need to build relationships in such a way that someone knows the needs of every child. Because students deserve every educator's best effort every day, there are no bad hair days for educators. The job is too important, and student learning is too important.

All educators must teach all children as if they are their own. Every child deserves a great education. Every child needs the knowledge, skills, and dispositions necessary for success in a new generation.

12. Educators must be transformational leaders

The field of leadership is inundated with books and articles defining leadership. Leaders should ask themselves what type of leader their school or school division needs: authentic, servant, situational, autocratic, visionary, entrepreneurial, laissez-faire, charismatic, transactional, or transformational? The literature challenges leaders to examine practices and to expand their knowledge, increase their skills, and examine their attitudes.

Though school leaders may fall into any one or a combination of the leadership types listed, emphasis will center on the last two, transactional and transformational leadership, as both are important to a school's success. Kotter (2012) provides an excellent comparison of transactional and transformational leaders as noted in table 10.1.

Of these two types of leadership, however, transformational must be considered the first among equals. Administrators must be change agents, viewing their roles as instructional and learning leaders as transformational. After every interaction, every faculty meeting, every observation, and every conference, teachers should leave with something that helps them become more effective. Missing an opportunity to help a teacher grow is missing an opportunity to improve student learning. Leithwood and Lewis (2012) identified two major ways in which building administrators impact student learning: creating a culture of achievement within the building, and motivating teachers. Both imply transformational leadership.

Table 10.1.

Transactional v. Transformational Leadership	
Manager	*Change Agent*
Planning and Budgeting	Establishing the direction by developing a vision of the future and strategies for producing changes needed to achieve the vision
Organizing and Staffing	Aligning people by communicating direction in words and deeds
Controlling and Problem Solving	Motivating and inspiring by energizing people to overcome political, bureaucratic, and resource barriers
Producing a degree of predictability and order with potential to produce short-term results	Producing change that people want

Chapter Ten

Transformational leaders utilize everything they know about instruction and learning to improve their schools. They focus on vision, the future, motivation, quality conversations, and producing change. It is this last component, producing change, which creates problems for many leaders. They often attempt change haphazardly without following a defined change process, a mistake because following a process for change increases the probability for success. While there are possible processes, the following process based around the *Breaking Ranks®* model is recommended.

The model of change begins with the assessment of appropriate data. Every school has access to a plethora of data. Sorting through the data, identifying the important data, and analyzing the data are important beginning steps. Some data will be more valuable than others and will become the foundation for creating an incentive for change.

Most people do not like change, preferring the status quo, sometimes even when the status quo is not working. So, for teachers, parents, students, and the community to embrace the change, there has to exist an incentive for change. That incentive generally will not come from international, national, and state data about the need to improve. It is also

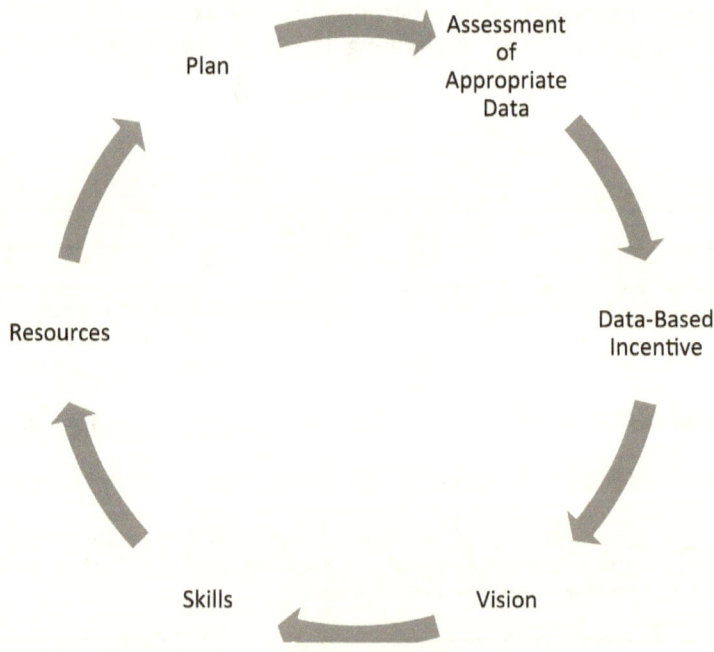

Figure 10.1.

unlikely that a school division will create an incentive for change. The incentive must be based on data at the individual school and individual teacher level.

It is only when data is drilled down to the lowest level possible that some people will see the need for change. Drilling down the data and creating the incentive will likely lead to most people buying into the change; however, this step may not bring everybody on board. Nonetheless, it should populate the bus with more people for the journey to school improvement. Principals cannot, however, wait for everyone to get on the bus. If the data demonstrates an urgent need, the sense of urgency overrides lack of commitment from everyone in the school. Principals must utilize the critical mass of supporters to begin the process of change.

Once the incentive is created and understood, the recommended change must be connected to the vision. There are two aspects of vision that are important. One is obvious: the change must be connected to the vision of the school and how it will help the school community reach its vision. The second, less obvious, link to vision, and the one most often overlooked, is how the change impacts personally each member of the school community.

Leaders must be clear and honest about how the change affects others. If the change affects teaching schedules, time commitments, professional responsibilities, or any number of other things, it should be communicated honestly to all. Telling members of the school community that the change will have limited effect in an effort to get their support will come back to haunt the leader if the change has a significant, unexpected impact. Members of the school community expect and respect honesty.

The next step in the change process is determining the skill set of the individuals connected to the change. The school leader must determine and plan the skill set necessary to implement the change and plan professional development as needed. If the proposed change is moving from a seven-period day to a block schedule, teachers must have the skill set to teach for 1.5 hours a day with the same content. If the change is writing across the curriculum, teachers in non-English areas must know enough to teach writing within their content areas. In both scenarios, professional development is essential.

Identifying whether or not resources are available to implement the change is the next step. If there is energy and support for implementing a new software program, but there are not enough technology resources to implement the change effectively, teachers lose interest.

The final step in the change process is development of a plan. How will the change be implemented? What is the time frame? Who will be responsible? How will it be evaluated? All of these are questions that are answered by a quality plan.

Educators who follow this change process are more likely to create the change that is needed. Failure to follow a process can be catastrophic.

> *Progress is impossible without change; and those who cannot change their minds cannot change anything.*
>
> —*George Bernard Shaw*

Eleven

Five Levels of Listening and Qualities of Effective Feedback

School leaders should choose a day and spend it intentionally focused on watching how people listen. People who do this are amazed at what they observe. Covey (1990) identified five levels of listening. As principals work with teachers and as teachers work with students, powerful conversations are very important to the teaching and learning process. If educators do not consciously improve their ability to listen, it will be hard to have powerful conversations.

This focus on listening is not a teaching strategy—it is a leadership strategy. All educators need to examine how well they listen. When teachers come to talk, do principals multitask or do they put down what they are doing and truly listen? Examining listening skills seriously is an important, but often overlooked, component of school improvement. Learning from others is valuable, but to do so requires real listening skills. Covey's Five Levels of Listening are briefly noted below.

FIVE LEVELS OF LISTENING

Level 1: Ignoring

This phase of listening is exactly what it implies. Individuals simply ignore what is being said. They continue to do what they were doing and demonstrate no desire to hear what the person is saying.

Level 2: Pretending

Some people pretend to listen. They may nod in agreement, make an occasional utterance such as "good," "I see," or "makes sense," but it is obvious they are not listening. They want people to think they are listening, but they are not.

Level 3: Selective

Some people are good at selective listening. They hear only pieces of a conversation. When this happens, they think they hear but end up taking things out of context. This often creates huge misunderstandings and communication problems.

Level 4: Attentive

Attentive listening is when people are truly listening. It appears they are hearing and understanding what is being said. They provide feedback and often paraphrase what the speaker is saying. An attentive listener clearly understands what is being said.

Level 5: Empathic

Empathic listening is the highest level of listening. Educators are able to step back, put aside their own feelings and beliefs, and listen without judgment. Empathic listeners rephrase comments to ensure they have heard something correctly. They will clarify or seek clarification for anything they are unsure of.

Empathic listening leads to developing trust, an important element of leadership. In fact, Kouzes and Posner (2010) state that without trust, organizations will underperform. They further state that the amount of influence which followers will accept from the leader is determined by the perceived level of trust followers have with the leader. Listening empathically is one way to develop trust.

> *Empathic listening is listening with intent to understand. I mean seeking first to understand, to really understand. Empathic listening gets inside another person's frame of reference. You look out through it, you see the world the way they see the world, you understand their paradigm, you understand how they feel.*
>
> —Stephen R. Covey

Hattie (2011) and the National Institute of School Leadership (2013) advocate for effective feedback. There are several defined qualities that, when present, enhance the quality of feedback. As principals engage in conversations with faculty about student learning, it is wise to remember the qualities described in the following paragraphs.

Feedback must be given with the intent to help people become better at what they do. The feedback must be couched as the interpretation of the observer. It is not based on hearsay but on what was observed. The feedback should be delivered as close to when it was observed as possible. Providing feedback should also be based on the premise that people want to improve and become better at what they do.

The feedback must describe behavior. It should be specific and free of innuendo, speculation, or subjectivity. As the feedback is provided, principals need to dig deeper into what influences teachers to make the decisions they make. This may be accomplished through effective questioning. It is best to stay away from "why" questions because they often prompt a defensive response. Rather than asking "why did you make that decision?" observers could ask a number of other questions:

- What prompted you to make that decision?
- What results were you looking for?
- How did that decision help you reach the objective?

For newer and/or less experienced teachers, principals may want to be more directive. When teachers do not have the experience to delve deeply into the reasons they make decisions, it may be helpful to give two or three examples of how decisions could have been made more effectively. This gives teachers choices of ways to improve both instruction and learning.

All feedback must be authentic and candid. Both false praise and deliberately withholding praise have downsides. Objective feedback delivered honestly is the goal. As opportunities arise to ask questions, it is best to be intentional about digging deeper into instructional and learning decisions.

One way to accomplish this is through three-deep questioning. When teachers respond, dig deeper by asking the teacher a question that requires deeper analysis or thought. Having teachers move beyond superficial responses is the goal. For example, in an observation of a math teacher, the observer might ask the following "three deep questions" concerning the use of vocabulary:

- How did you feel about your use of math vocabulary during the lesson?
- What evidence do you have that students use math vocabulary appropriately?
- What could you have done differently during the lesson that would have required students to use the vocabulary?

Finally, feedback must stimulate action. If the feedback does not lead to improved performance, changes to instructional practices, or changes in behavior, it is of little use.

TWELVE
The School Improvement Process

School improvement is a continuous, never ending process. The process includes many components and when things are going well, many of the components are often overlooked. On the other hand, when things are not going well, the totality of school improvement seems daunting. Great principals realize there must be an intentional focus on what is important and understand how important each component of school improvement is to success.

The visual, "The School Improvement Process" identifies the components of school improvement.* It is important for principals to be intentional about each one. The visual can be a day-to-day reminder of the importance of intentionally focusing on what is important.

The first component is being intentional about the school improvement process. There are many resources to help in leading this effort. One of the best resources is available through the Center on Innovation and Improvement. Its website at www.centerii.org/, includes a wealth of free resources, strategies, and techniques connected to school improvement. Much of their work is connected to many state and school districts' efforts to improve schools.

So, if being intentional is the first step, about what should schools be intentional? Each of the elements will be identified and explained.

NON-NEGOTIABLE SET OF BELIEFS

As previously noted, there must be a set of non-negotiable beliefs that permeate the school. These should not be just a list of statements but true beliefs that underlie everything that is done in the school. Everyone in the school may be able to state the beliefs but for substantial school improvement, everyone must live the beliefs if student achievement is to improve.

The foundational beliefs will differ from school to school; however, there are some fundamental beliefs that should probably be in any list.

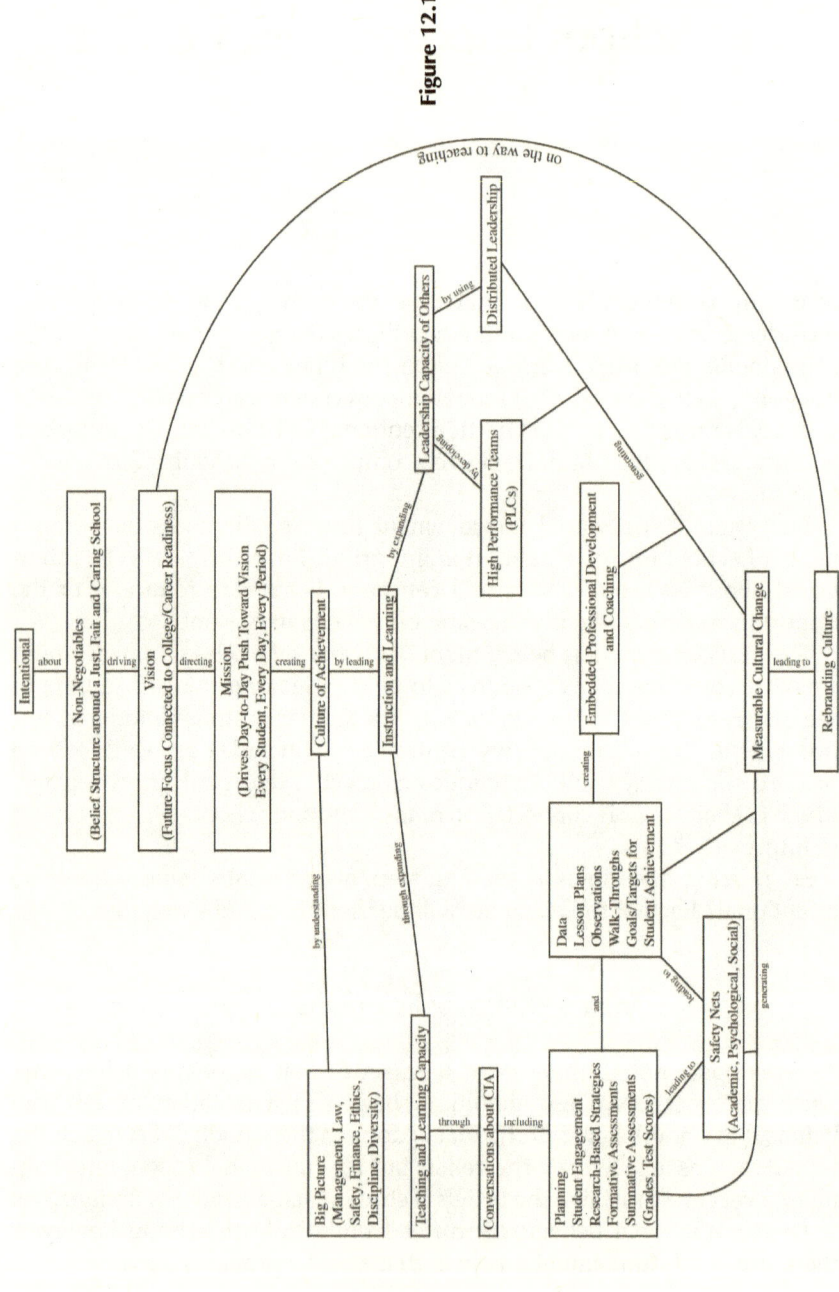

Figure 12.1.

The following foundational beliefs are shared as a beginning point for the important conversations that must occur in schools.

- Every child can learn.
- Every child is important.
- Every child has a gift.
- Every child should be challenged.
- Every child should be respected.
- Every child should be encouraged.
- Every child should get everyone's best effort every day.
- Every child deserves an outstanding principal and teacher.

Earlier in chapter 10, there was a discussion of the Essential Twelve. Those twelve principles, restated below, should also be considered as a part of the non-negotiable beliefs of the schools.

- Educators must be instructional and learning leaders.
- Effort and persistence lead to increased learning.
- Great teaching matters.
- Learning takes time but must lead to college and career ready graduates.
- High expectations promote learning.
- Vision, non-negotiables, and intentionality create a trifecta for success.
- Growth mindsets are a foundation for increased student learning.
- Motivation matters, intrinsic motivation matters more.
- Tight alignment of curriculum, instruction, and assessment makes a difference.
- Feedback must stimulate action.
- Every child, by need, every day.
- Educators must be transformational leaders.

Vision

From the above twenty statements, schools should be able to identify a set of beliefs that provide the foundation for the school vision. The vision is what connects the school to the future. While the Center for School Change advocates for charter schools, it does offer some good advice for vision statements by asking the following question: "If your school is extremely successful over the next three–five years, how will people describe your school? Think about the answer as you begin to develop the vision."

The school vision should drive decisions within the school. It should prepare students for options and for the future. It must recognize the value of every student, not just those who are college bound. The vision should reflect ambitious goals and provide direction for the school. As noted previously, *Breaking Ranks®* research notes that one of the greatest obstacles to school reform is the lack of a compelling vision.

There are numerous authors who have identified the traits of a vision statement. Most are very similar and note that a vision statement should be:

- Measurable (focused on results),
- Clear,
- Realistic,
- Attainable but stretches, and
- A living, breathing document.

The National Institute of School Leadership (NISL) adds a trait not included in other sources. NISL argues that the vision statement should be "worth fighting for."

Developing the vision is an important process and should not be taken lightly. Involving all stakeholders is important. Everyone should be involved in developing the vision, and everyone should be committed to the vision once developed. To some extent, developing a vision is comparable to creating a brand. It is how you want the community to see your school.

The Center for School Change (2013) includes sample vision statements on its website including the following.

- Our vision is to create a nationally known inner city elementary school that produces major gains in student achievement, and helps make the neighborhood in which it is located a much more pleasant place in which to live and work.
- Our vision is to create one of the state's most effective schools helping secondary students who have not succeeded in traditional schools, prepare for, and be accepted into, post-secondary education.
- Our vision is to create an extremely effective K–8 rural school that not only produces very high levels of student achievement, but also helps train the next generation of rural teachers.
- Our vision is to create a K–12 school that is highly regarded for its academic excellence, and for its contribution in actively serving and improving the community in which it operates.

The Center for School Change adds that "a vision is more than broad, flowery statements. The vision helps people understand how you hope others will view you, and describes some of your highest priorities."

Mission

While the vision identifies the future, a mission statement is helpful in driving the day-to-day push toward implementing the vision. It should reflect the basic beliefs within the school and help everyone move toward the vision. In essence, the mission statement should focus on every student, every day, every period.

Mission statements are not long. They may even be considered to be slogans that highlight the daily mission of the school. The mission statement should be a simple statement or slogan that is a consistent reminder of the underlying non-negotiable beliefs of the school community and where the school is heading. A few examples follow:

- Inspire a love of learning and celebrate achievement.
- Cultivate a love of learning in every child.
- Inspire a passion for learning.
- Graduate college and career ready.

Core beliefs, vision, and mission are closely connected. None of the three should stand alone. All three are necessary components of school improvement. Being intentional about the core beliefs (non-negotiables), vision, and mission should help create a culture that focuses on student achievement and student learning. Leithwood and Lewis (2012) note that one of the two most significant ways that principals impact student learning is through creating a culture that includes student achievement and student learning as its top priority.

* Thanks to Jacque Gibble, National Institute of School Leadership trainer, who provided valuable feedback about the school improvement model.

Thirteen

Creating a Culture of Achievement

Creating a culture of achievement includes several components including understanding the big picture and intentionally leading instruction and learning. School leaders need to have the ability to see the big picture. They need to see the perspective from the federal, state, local, and school levels. Leaders cannot get so caught up in the day-to-day operations that they lose sight of bigger issues.

BIG PICTURE THINKING

At the school level, it is also important to see the big picture of what is going on within the building. Leaders need to pay particular attention to management issues, making sure that policies and procedures are implemented and followed. Failure to manage effectively may well lead to chaos. Management is important, but leaders manage so they can lead. Management is about process and procedures, leadership is about taking the school where it needs to go.

Leaders must also have a solid foundation and understanding of legal issues. Creating safe and caring schools requires an understanding of legal issues including, among others, freedom of speech, freedom of religion, search and seizure, due process, bullying, and cyberbullying.

Some principals make bad decisions because they do not understand legal issues. When this happens, it takes the focus away from student achievement and school improvement. While it is important from an administrative viewpoint to know what one cannot do in relation to the law, it is more important to view the law as a guide for rational and fair action. The law is one of the many lenses through which we reflect upon our policies and practices.

A solid legal foundation also provides an avenue for making ethical decisions in schools. Elias (2013) made the following observation: "The best educational leaders touch the heart as well as the mind and appeal to deep values, rather than relying on research findings." Elias goes on to argue that school leaders should promote "human dignity." Creating ethical schools means making hard choices and decisions that are in the best interest of student achievement.

Pink (2010) argues that most people are motivated by three things: autonomy, mastery, and purpose. Purpose means being connected to something bigger than themselves. For some, that will take a religious significance, for others a moral or ethical significance. Perhaps school leaders can motivate by helping teachers, staff, students, and parents focus on a purpose bigger than themselves by constantly drawing attention to the school vision and mission that focus on the importance of every child.

> *The ultimate measure of a man is not where he stands in moments of comfort, but where he stands at times of challenge and controversy.*
>
> —Martin Luther King, Jr.

One way to focus on ethical schools and positive school discipline is to link both to character education programs. According to the Character Education Partnership (www.character.com), eighteen states mandate character education programs. Another eighteen states encourage such programs. An additional seven states support character education initiatives but without any specific legislation. That leaves only seven states that do not make any reference to character education. States more than likely have goals similar to those noted in § 22.1-208.01 of the *Code of Virginia*. Character education programs "shall be to instill in students civic virtues and personal character traits so as to improve the learning environment, promote student achievement, reduce disciplinary problems, and develop civic-minded students of high character."

The Virginia legislation includes a list of traits which may be taught. These include the following: "(1) trustworthiness, including honesty, integrity, reliability, and loyalty; (2) respect, including the precepts of the Golden Rule, tolerance, and courtesy; (3) responsibility, including hard work, economic self-reliance, accountability, diligence, perseverance, and self-control; (4) fairness, including justice, consequences of bad behavior, principles of nondiscrimination, and freedom from prejudice; (5) caring, including kindness, empathy, compassion, consideration, generosity, and charity; and (6) citizenship, including patriotism, the Pledge of Allegiance, respect for the American flag, concern for the common good, respect for authority and the law, and community-mindedness." The program must also address the inappropriateness of bullying.

Palestini (2012) noted that Horace Mann, considered by many to be the father of American public education, advocated for such character traits. Mann believed that these traits would provide a moral compass based on a philosophy that was compatible with all religions.

What better way to implement a character education program, already required or encouraged in a majority of states, than to link it to a school's discipline program. If everyone in a school was intentional about these character traits, discipline might improve. Every discipline issue in a school will link to one or more of the identified character traits.

Administrators and teachers would have an avenue to discuss student decisions around these character traits. Of course, there are two philosophies to school discipline: to punish or to change behavior. If a school's purpose is to change behavior, helping students link their decisions to the defined character traits may become one of those "teachable moments."

Certainly, the requirement to address bullying can be linked to the character traits. Rather than focusing on the negative actions of the bully, why not ask the bully to share how their behavior connected to the identified character traits? Why not engage students in discussions about their behavior and how those decisions affect character? Is it possible that by refocusing on positive character traits, students may reframe their thinking?

In addition, such an emphasis would allow administrators a "door way" to have conversations about cyberbullying which occurs off school grounds. While the courts have been reluctant to allow school administrators to discipline students for "off-grounds speech," there is no deterrent to having conversations about such speech. Even without disciplining a student, having the student think about his or her behavior in the context of character traits may be helpful.

Diversity issues are also very important in big picture thinking. Creating a school environment where students, parents, and faculty from different backgrounds and experiences can work together is an important aspect of public education. Prejudice, discrimination, racism, and stereotyping all get in the way of creating a culture of achievement.

School leaders need to model behaviors that promote acceptance of diversity within their schools. Leaders need to remember that diversity means more than race. It is related to, among other things, gender, socioeconomic status, disability, and religion. Leaders must value and respect all who come to learn within the walls of the school. School leaders must model acceptance. They must make decisions based on facts not assumptions. School leaders must be intentional about modeling behavior that promotes the importance of diversity.

Fourteen

Instruction and Learning

School leaders must lead instruction and learning. They must expand the teaching and learning capacity of both teachers and students through conversations that focus on planning, student engagement, research-based (high yield) teaching strategies, formative assessments, summative assessments, data, lesson plans, goals/targets for student achievement, and observations and evaluations.

Instructional and learning leadership are addressed earlier in this book and will not be repeated. However, there are several additional aspects of instruction and learning that will be addressed. These include use of data, observation and evaluation feedback, plans of assistance, and safety nets.

USE OF DATA

While teachers need to gather data about individual students, data also needs to be collected around school improvement. Bernhardt (2003) argues that most any question about schools can be answered through the use of four kinds of data. She defines those data points as demographic data, student learning data, perceptual data, and school processes data.

In most schools, a lot of data is gathered. Some of the data is valuable, some not so much. Leaders need to examine the types of data gathered and determine when it is gathered, how it is used, and the impact of the data on school improvement. Time is valuable and should be wisely spent on examining useful data.

Bernhardt (2003) describes demographic data as describing the context in which the school operates. This data allows information to be disaggregated by gender, race, socioeconomic, disability, limited English proficiency, and a host of other factors. This data is very valuable to put all other school data in context.

Student learning data includes measures that demonstrate the impact of teaching and learning on students within the school. They include teacher-made tests, formative assessments, district-based assessments, grades, criterion-referenced tests (including state assessments), norm-referenced assessments (including IQ tests, Stanford 9, Iowa Test of Basic Skills), and a variety of authentic assessments.

Perceptual data helps leaders understand how stakeholders view and perceive the school or district. The results may be real or perceived, but for the stakeholders who provide the information, perception is reality. This data is gathered through surveys, questionnaires, observations, and interviews. If schools choose not to create a brand for the school, perceptual data will enable leaders to see what brand stakeholders have put on the school. This data can be very helpful.

School process data is a delineation of processes and programs operating within the school or district. It includes how various aspects of the school including instruction, curriculum, assessment, attendance, discipline, transportation, athletics, and extracurriculars are implemented. It includes policies, procedures, and practices. This data is often overlooked in school improvement but can provide valuable information. For example, there are times when attendance or discipline policies have negative impacts on student learning. Without examining such policies, the real reason for the problem may go unnoticed.

OBSERVATIONS, EVALUATIONS, AND PLANS OF ASSISTANCE

Another element of instruction and learning not referenced earlier is the ability of school leaders to be effective observers and evaluators. Whether using walk throughs, formal observations, or clinical supervision, it is important to create a culture where the focus is on everyone in the school becoming better at what they do, including the school leaders.

School leaders must provide feedback to teachers through the observation and evaluation process. The feedback needs to be useful and should help teachers become more effective. School leaders are encouraged to review the feedback they have provided teachers in the past. In many cases, the language of the feedback is the same for all teachers. A superintendent should be able to read ten observations of ten different teachers and tell whether or not the teachers are superstars, average, or below average. If he or she cannot, the written feedback is of little value.

It is also important for school leaders to be able to write an effective plan of assistance for teachers who need it. Observations and evaluations should focus on the professionalization of teachers with the expectations that teachers are responsible for improving their own knowledge and skill set as well as constantly examining their own attitudes. The role of the school leader is to provide feedback to help the teacher become more effective which in turn leads to increased student learning.

As part of the evaluation process, make sure that teachers have been given clear standards and expectations for performance. All professionals should know what is expected and what school leaders are looking for when they are in a classroom.

The evaluation document should emphasize the importance of student achievement and/or student academic progress. It should also establish a common vocabulary around instruction. When school leaders reference formative assessment, for example, every teacher should know exactly what formative assessment means.

A plan of assistance should be based on evidence that clearly identifies a problem. Some plans are nothing more than a list of activities to be completed by the teacher. When the teacher completes everything on the plan, they are no longer under the plan. Solving the problem must be the heart of the plan of assistance. If the plan does not help the teacher solve the problem, it is not the fault of the plan.

Do not make statements like "the plan was not successful in correcting your unsatisfactory performance." It is the teacher's responsibility to solve the problem. If the problem remains, continue documentation to terminate.

SAFETY NETS

As previously noted, effort is important; however, effort alone will not be enough for all students. Students have different resources including levels of prior learning, parental support, and financial resources. As Dweck (2006) notes, effort is a condition for success, but educators must provide support and safety nets.

In the school improvement process, it is important for leaders to recognize the importance of safety nets for students. Safety nets are strategies that support students who are struggling. Generally, leaders think about academic safety nets including remediation, after school programs, Saturday school, computer software programs, credit recovery, summer school, intersessions or a number of other strategies. These safety nets are important.

As school leaders focus on continuous improvement efforts, it is important to address the three major indicators: achievement, attendance, and discipline. It is important to track each individual student in each of these areas. Intervention needs to occur at defined times. Intervention cannot be a choice; it must be a mandate.

Schools cannot rely solely on teachers to identify students for intervention nor can they rely on students or parents to make that identification. There must be a defined trigger in each of these three areas that mandates that students receive intervention services.

It is critical for school leaders to define the trigger in each area that leads to intervention or use of a safety net. These triggers may vary from school to school, but they need to be present. Examples of achievement triggers include making a D or F for the grading period, a particular score on a benchmark assessment, reading inventory scores, teacher-made test scores, or failing a state or end-of-course assessment.

Attendance triggers may be based on a defined number of absences or tardies. These absences/tardies may be related to school attendance or class attendance.

Discipline triggers may be based on a specific number of referrals, getting a referral from two or more teachers, number of in-school suspensions, number of detentions, or number of suspensions.

Obviously, there are many other triggers which could be identified for each indicator. What is important is that each school has defined triggers for each of these three areas that result in mandated intervention.

While students who are struggling or below grade level need the opportunity to catch up to their peers, it is important for leaders to assess the quality of the academic safety nets. All initiatives need to be evaluated for effectiveness on a regular basis. Is the safety net working? Are teachers seeing increased student achievement as a result of students participating in the safety net initiative? If not, leaders need to look for other strategies and safety nets that do help students academically.

While academic safety nets are important, it is just as important to create social and psychological safety nets. Both of these types of safety nets are connected to the personalization of schools clearly noted as important in *Breaking Ranks®: The Comprehensive Framework for School Improvement*.

Social safety nets are important because students need to feel safe at school. Discipline and its link to character education issues were addressed earlier. In addition, it is important for school leaders to analyze discipline data to ensure that all students are being treated equitably. Are subgroups of students (minority, disabled, free lunch) being referred and/or suspended at higher rates? If so, what is being done?

It is easy to react to discipline issues. However, in schools with strong psychological and social safety nets, leaders go much deeper into discipline issues. They look at the number of referrals by teacher as well as where the behavior occurred that led to the referral, i.e., classroom, cafeteria, playground, hallways, bus, or outside as well as the time of the referral, i.e., before school, after school, morning, or after lunch.

A root cause analysis must be done in an effort to get to the cause of the behavior so that assistance can be provided to the student. This does not mean there are no consequences to the behavior, only that school leaders are working to change behavior of the student rather than punish him.

RECOGNITION AND ACCEPTANCE

Recognition and acceptance are two important relationships identified in *Breaking Ranks®* that are important in developing personalized schools. These relationships are also directly connected to the importance of creating social and psychological safety nets. Leaders should consider the student needs connected to these relationships as well as the school practices to ensure there is congruence.

For example, students need to find and have a voice within the school environment. This does not necessarily mean they need more freedom of speech; instead, it means that students need to begin finding out who they are, what they are good at, and how they can be involved in ways that promote their voice and that promote who they are.

School policies and practices around recognition should promote equity. Are different types of students recognized in meaningful ways? Does all the recognition go to the scholars or the athletes? Recognizing scholars and athletes is important, but what about students who have a different talent or gift?

Are students who are involved in career technical programs recognized? What about students in theater, drama, forensics, or music? What about students involved in community activities? Students need to be recognized and valued for who they are. They need to be connected to an adult they can see themselves becoming. They need to be known by their teachers.

As Theodore Sizer (1999) noted, "We cannot teach students well if we do not know them well" (p. 6). When leaders and teachers in the school know their students well, it helps create those social and psychological safety nets.

Acceptance is also an important relationship. Students have a need to belong to something. Leaders need to figure out ways to help students belong. Leaders need to ensure that policies and practices create a sense of community within schools. If students do not feel accepted within positive environments, they will gravitate toward negative environments. In the end, they will put themselves in an environment where they are accepted.

EMBEDDED PROFESSIONAL DEVELOPMENT

As leaders work to improve schools, it is important to determine the type of professional development experiences needed within the school. Since each school has its own DNA, it is important to determine the types of professional development through analysis of school data and feedback from teachers. One-size-fits-all initiatives at the school division/district level are less likely to produce meaningful experiences that inform instruction and learning.

Professional development is a critical aspect of school improvement. Embedding professional development around the day-to-day operations of the school may be more valuable than pulling teachers out of the classroom for day-long professional development.

In addition, leaders are under increased financial pressures to cut budgets, and one of the areas where budgets are cut is professional development. Thus, leaders may need to think "inside the box" rather than outside the box when designing such experiences. Leaders need to ask themselves "what resources do we have within the building to provide professional development?" What role can the "superstar" teachers play in providing training? Can professional learning communities (PLC) play a larger role?

Perhaps each teacher in a PLC can study one research-based (high yield) instructional strategy, try the strategy with her students, and report the results to other teachers in the PLC. If all teachers do this, there is an opportunity to expand the teaching and learning capacity of all teachers. There is no cost to do this, and it has been accomplished by thinking within the school or "within the box."

In creating professional development opportunities for teachers, it is important to consider principles of adult learning. There are numerous theories related to adult learning which leaders should consider.

In his theory of andragogy, Knowles (2008) argues there are six principles of adult learning which need to be considered. These principles include the following:

- Adults are internally motivated and self-directed
- Adults bring life experiences and knowledge to learning experiences
- Adults are goal oriented
- Adults are relevancy oriented
- Adults are practical
- Adult learners like to be respected

Leaders should consider the above six principles when designing professional development.

In his theory of self-directed learning Tough (1971) states that adults engage in systematic learning as part of their everyday activities. He argues that leaders should foster self-directed learning. In designing professional development experiences, leaders may benefit from creating a structure where teachers are encouraged to take the new information, internalize it, and apply within their own classroom.

Cranton (2006) supports this approach by stating that teachers should make their own assumptions about effective teaching, engage in conversation with others, reflect on their assumptions, and develop an informed theory of practice. This is exactly what leaders are trying to get teachers to do through embedded professional development.

Brown, Collins, and Duguid (1989) provide additional support for embedded professional development through their theory of situated cognition. Lasting knowledge emerges when learners engage in authentic activity embedded in specific situations. Teachers increase their knowledge by being immersed in real situations, with support from experienced colleagues who use modeling and coaching strategies to reinforce the new learning.

Just as teachers need to differentiate instruction for students, leaders need to consider strategies to differentiate professional development for teachers. Sternberg (1995) argues that leaders need to individualize teacher learning. New teachers need to be supervised differently than experienced teachers. For both new and experienced teachers, Sternberg states that teachers must focus on adding effective instructional strategies to change the classroom environment and improve student learning. This is best accomplished through collaborative activities and reflection.

Whatever the professional development entails, it is important to create a structure that ensures implementation. Such a structure can take many forms, but it must ensure implementation of the new idea, resource, or strategy. This can be accomplished through a variety of structures including collegial supervision, teachers observing other teachers, formal observations, informal observations, walk throughs, or required conversations in PLC's.

Reiss (2007) discussed the need to help teachers abandon the comfort zone. She provided an illustration similar to the one below noting the

Figure 14.1.

importance of helping others abandon the comfortable and safe environment and helping them move to a future state where anything is possible. Doing this requires teachers to get through the discomfort zone.

Leaders have to help teachers deal with the doubt and fear of doing something different. They have to be very intentional about providing support and assistance during this time. Focusing on the underlying beliefs and vision of the school can help teachers move into the zone where anything is possible.

Fifteen
Expanding the Leadership Capacity of Others

In addition to expanding teaching and learning capacity, leaders must also focus on expanding the leadership capacity of others. Two areas of importance in accomplishing this task include developing high performance teams and using distributed leadership.

HIGH PERFORMANCE TEAMS

Katzenbach and Smith (2003) noted there are five distinct teams that emerge in organizations. These teams include a working group, pseudo-team, potential team, real team, and high performance team. Working groups rely on "individual bests." Pseudo-teams are groups of individuals who call themselves a team but do not take risks to solve problems nor do they develop joint work-products: they are the lowest performing teams. Potential teams are groups of individuals who do take risks to solve problems, and they develop joint work products. They work hard to solve problems; however, they often encounter obstacles and are not able to overcome them unless good leadership emerges.

The top two teams, as defined by Katenbach and Smith (2003), are real teams and high performing teams. Real teams are composed of individuals committed to a common purpose and who hold themselves accountable for results. They make significant contributions to the school.

High performance teams are real teams where members are committed to helping the school and each other grow and succeed. There is a real commitment to the school and to each other. Real teams help the school, grade level, unit, or department get better. High performance teams help all of these as well as each other get better.

Many schools utilize professional learning communities (PLCs) as a strategy to develop more effective teams. PLCs can be a great avenue to accomplish this; however, leaders must remember that PLCs are structural changes, not cultural changes. Leaders have to change the culture of the school regarding teams in order to have meaningful involvement.

Dufour (2008), one of the gurus of PLCs, emphatically states that members of PLCs must be committed to working together to achieve a collective purpose. Members must develop a collaborative culture. He goes on to state that high performing PLCs must assess effectiveness on the basis of results, not intentions. They must focus around a culture of continuous improvement and must rely on appropriate data to assess effectiveness.

> *Coming together is a beginning, staying together is progress and working together is success.*
>
> —Henry Ford

Developing and supporting high performance teams and PLCs is one part of expanding the leadership capacity of others. The second part is effectively using distributed leadership. School or division leaders cannot do it all. They must rely on others to help—both administrators and teachers.

DISTRIBUTED LEADERSHIP

Some leaders believe that if they distribute leadership they will lose some of their ability to lead. Leithwood and Lewis (2012) noted that the exact opposite is the result of distributed leadership. When leaders give leadership away, they are seen as more effective leaders.

Effective use of distributed leadership, however, does not just happen. It has to be cultivated and modeled. Kelley (1992) wrote about the importance of developing effective followers. He noted that leadership is often taught, but followership is not.

> *Look over your shoulder every now and then to make sure someone is following you.*
>
> —Henry Gilmer

Kouzes and Posner (2010) make the point that leadership starts with the leader, but continues only if there are followers. Leadership emerges when someone willingly follows the leader. Leadership is really about persuasion.

These authors also make the case that leaders cannot do it alone. They have to develop followers. They argue that this is done by building relationships, listening emphatically, uniting followers around a shared vision and sharing how the vision connects to each follower, and by convincing followers of their potential.

Kouzes and Posner further state that the level of trust followers have for the leader determines the amount of influence followers will accept. Thus, the greater the trust, the greater the ability of the leader to persuade followers to move in a particular direction.

Their research also suggests that challenge is the crucible for greatness. There is a great quote by Randy Pausch in his book, *The Last Lecture* (2008): "Brick walls are there for a reason. They are not there to keep us out. . . . [They are] there to give us a chance to show how badly we want something" (p. 79).

Leaders must have a deep connection with the people they lead. Kouzes and Posner note that the highest performing leaders are the most open and caring. They further state that leaders do not seek the attention of others, they give it to others. The size of the gesture is not as important as the fact that leaders notice someone's contribution.

There is also some interesting work by Robert Kelley (1992) about followers. Leaders have to develop the capacity of others to lead. According to Kelley, effective leaders have the vision to set goals, interpersonal skills to reach consensus, verbal capacity to communicate enthusiasm to diverse groups, organizational talent to coordinate disparate efforts, and the desire to lead.

Effective followers have the vision to see the forest and the trees, the social capacity to work with others, strength of character to flourish without heroic status, moral and psychological balance to pursue personal and corporate goals at no cost to either, and the desire to participate in a team effort to accomplish a common purpose.

Kelley further argues that leaders should not assume that everyone knows how to follow. This assumption is based on three faulty premises: leaders are more important than followers; following is just doing what you are told; and followers draw their energy and aims from the leader. Instead, Kelley argues that leaders should focus on helping followers to: self manage their behaviors; align personal goals and commitments to those of the organization; and act responsibly toward the organization, the leader, coworkers, and oneself.

The following chart illustrates the types of followers that exist within organizations, including schools.

The goal of the leader is to have followers who are independent critical thinkers. Having these individuals will help the organization improve. However, all followers are not independent critical thinkers. There are many other types of followers who have to be encouraged, motivated,

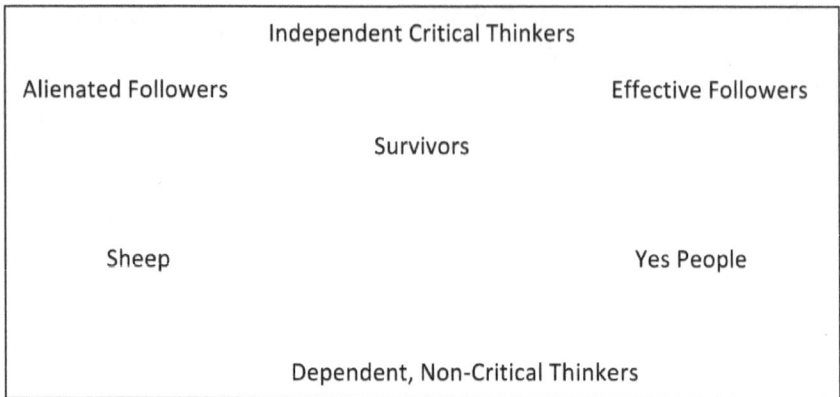

Figure 15.1.

and coached to get to the point where they have the greatest impact on the organization.

Some followers are dependent, noncritical thinkers. They want to be told what to do. Other followers are sheep, they go wherever the leader directs them; they will never challenge what the leader wants to do. In addition, they rarely express their point of view.

Some followers are yes people. They may express their positions, but they want to please so they agree to everything the leader wants to do even when they know it is wrong. Pleasing is more important than organizational effectiveness.

Survivors are those followers who do whatever they need to do to get through the day. They exhibit the mindset of "this too shall pass." They will do just enough to make it look like they want the organization to be successful.

The alienated followers may be independent thinkers, but their thinking is not in line with where the organization is heading. These followers are often the most difficult to embrace. They are generally passive—they think but do not act. They are cynics who consciously or unconsciously undermine what goes on within the organization.

The effective followers assume responsibility for their behavior and its impact on the organization. They are not afraid to draw the leader's attention to behavior that is hurting the organization.

> *If leaders are moving forward and look back to see no one following them, they are hiking not leading.*
>
> —Roger Jones

Leaders need to focus on helping followers become independent critical thinkers. Leaders need to model, support, and encourage behavior that promotes critical thinking. They need to expect and require followers to honor the beliefs, vision, and mission of the school. They must expect teachers to consistently improve their own teaching and student learning.

Leaders should expect all within the school to embody all of the elements of effective instruction, learning, and school improvement. Expecting and requiring everyone to act in the best interests of students may spur some in the right direction. Behavioral change often precedes attitudinal change.

During National Institute of School Leadership (NISL) training, presenters attributed the following quote to Richard Elmore: "Grab people by their actions, and their beliefs will follow." Insist that teachers and staff act in ways that create the type of school culture that leads to increased student achievement.

Sixteen
Establishing Cultural Change and Rebranding

Change is necessary for school improvement. Some leaders, when asked to describe change, use descriptors including words like hard, difficult, time-consuming, necessary, challenging, and any number of other adjectives.

While these descriptors may be true, they do not help leaders understand how to implement change. Most leaders do not think of change as a process, but it is. Unless leaders intentionally think about a process of change, they will be less likely to implement sustainable change.

Leaders often use the terms culture and climate synonymously, but they are not synonyms. For the sake of this discussion, culture relates to decisions made within the school. It includes the tangible items that leaders can look to. Items such as the underlying beliefs of the school, vision, mission, goals, traditions, and how discipline is administered help to create the culture.

Climate, on the other hand, is how faculty, students, parents, and community feel about the culture. How do they really feel about being in the school? Do they feel valued and respected? Climate is often determined by the use of perceptual data.

Leaders often make the mistake of believing that change is implemented through changing the structure. They often believe that creating PLCs, block schedules, career academies or changing an attendance or grading policy will improve schools. These are structural changes, and while they are important, they do not necessarily change the culture of a school.

Meaningful and sustainable change is best implemented with a cultural change. These are changes to the underlying beliefs and vision within the school. For example, Jones and Wheeler (2011) found that schools making significant standards-based gains did so by implementing cultural change.

Principals of those schools had to make changes to the vision and mission or they had to create a culture where everyone lived the vision and mission. They examined curriculum, instruction, and assessment and realized there was little real alignment so they had to undertake an analysis of why that was true. In doing so, they changed the culture which resulted in a tighter alignment.

Hattie (2011) states that changing the culture of the school is the essence of sustained improvement. Leaders must realize that structural change is not cultural change. Culture always trumps structure!

There are numerous theories and models around change. Leaders should use whichever model helps them become intentional about the process of change.

Since the culture of a school is frozen, it will not change without a reason. An early model of change developed by Kurt Lewin (1947) describes change in three phases. The first phase is unfreezing existing mindsets. The second phase is initiating and implementing the change. He notes this stage includes periods of confusion and challenge. Leaders have to shepherd faculty, staff, students, and parents through this phase. The third phase is freezing the change and making it a part of existing culture.

Thinking about Lewin's model of unfreezing, implementing, and freezing may be an effective way to approach change. However, the model does not describe how the leader should actually implement the model.

Two models which may be helpful in implementing sustainable change are the *Breaking Ranks®* model and Kotter's (2012) eight-stage process of change. Each may be helpful to leaders.

Breaking Ranks® recommends a five-stage process: incentive, vision, skills, resources, and plan. Create an incentive to change, perhaps by using Bernhardt's (2003) four types of data referenced in chapter 15: demographic data, student learning data, perceptual data, and school process data.

Leaders must connect the change to the underlying beliefs, vision, and mission of the school. They must also connect the change to individual teachers so teachers know how the change affects them.

Leaders must determine whether or not teachers and staff have the skill set to implement the change. If not, professional development must be provided.

If there are no resources to implement the change, the change will fail. Examining resources must occur before change is implemented.

Finally, there must be a plan to implement the change. That plan must include details to implement, monitor, evaluate, and sustain the change.

Kotter (2012) advocates for an eight-stage process and many leaders have found it successful. The eight stages include the following:

- Establish a sense of urgency.
- Create a guiding coalition.

- Develop a vision and strategy.
- Communicate the change vision.
- Empower employees for broad-based action.
- Generate short-term wins.
- Consolidate gains and produce more change.
- Anchor new approaches in the culture.

Kotter's eight-stage process is similar to the five-phase process of *Breaking Ranks®*. It is more important to identify and follow a change process than to argue that one process is better than another. Leaders should examine a variety of processes and follow one best suited to their school.

Implementing sustainable change is about changing the culture. Squire and Reigeluth, (2000) note that the most important outcome of any significant change must be a change in the stakeholders' mindsets and beliefs about education. Without changes in mindsets, no fundamental change is likely to succeed or be sustained.

In many ways, changing the culture of a school is a form of branding. Every school has its own DNA and every school has its own brand. Often that brand is established by those outside the school, either intentionally or unintentionally. If schools do not intentionally create their own brand, others will create one for them.

Private schools often do a much better job of creating a brand, of describing their niche and what they do well. Public schools might learn something from that approach through being intentional about creating sustainable change and rebranding their own culture.

Seventeen

Final Thoughts

Instructional leadership, learning leadership, and school improvement leadership are critical components of educational leadership. School leaders have a responsibility to students and the school community to help students grow and learn every day. They have a challenging yet rewarding job: to teach the next generation of workers and leaders. It is a responsibility that requires them to push students to excellence and to convince students they can do something they did not believe they could do.

> You are not a teacher until you can reach inside the minds of children and convince them that they can do something they did not believe they could do. Until then, you are a placeholder.
>
> —Unknown

The visual models are presented as a first step in challenging school leaders to think about, discuss, and reflect on those things that impact teaching, learning, and school improvement. The intent is to encourage educational leaders to have quality conversations around things that matter and which increase student achievement.

Perhaps the most critical aspect of educational leadership is that leaders have to want to lead. Leaders have to be passionate about leading, increasing student learning, and school improvement. They need to develop a curiosity for why things are the way they are even to the point of conducting a root cause analysis to get to the real issues.

> Your PQ (passion quotient) and your CG (curiosity quotient) are more important than your IQ (intelligence quotient).
>
> —Dick Flanary

Leaders have to be willing to be accountable and to use accountability as a motivator. They must work to create a culture where student learning is the primary goal. Leaders must also be focused on the future—focused on the vision.

Leaders have to be authentic. They have to be themselves, not emulate the leadership style of someone else. Leaders need to expand their knowledge, improve their skills, and challenge their attitudes on a regular basis. They have to earn the right to lead. You earn that right through being yourself.

> What lies behind us and what lies before us are tiny matters compared to what lies within us.
>
> —Ralph Waldo Emerson

Inspiring others is a quality of an outstanding educational leader. As Goffee and Jones (2006) note, leaders need to capture the heart, mind, and soul. They have to care intensely about the work of their faculty and staff. Leaders have to care about everyone in the school: every child, every parent, every teacher, every employee is important, and leaders need to act accordingly.

Leaders should not be ashamed, as Goffee and Jones note, to reveal their humanity. They should capitalize on their own uniqueness. Leaders bring a personality and a skill set to the job. Do not be afraid to use either one.

Manage the school well. Policies, procedures, regulations, and rules exist for a reason. Use them, but make sure they have been examined and are congruent with the underlying beliefs, vision, and mission of the school. Managing well gives leaders more time to lead.

> Management is doing things right; leadership is doing the right things.
>
> —Peter Drucker

Transformational leaders create change that benefits the school. Understanding the change process is a critical piece of leadership. Cultural change does not just happen. It is possible to implement a structural change without much thought—establish a block schedule, change a policy, create a dress code, adopt a new text, or purchase a new software program. Those are structural changes, not cultural changes.

Final Thoughts

Leaders have to change the culture of a school. Cultural change comes through planning for change. Whether that planning is based on *Breaking Ranks®*, Kotter's eight steps, or some other change process is less important than planning for change and being prepared for the unintended consequences and being prepared for those who will try to block the change.

> Change is the law of life and those who look only to the past or present are certain to miss the future.
>
> —John F. Kennedy

As simplistic as it sounds, school leaders must focus on the trifecta of school improvement: vision, intentionality, and non-negotiables. Stay grounded in the underlying non-negotiable beliefs that drive the school. Be very intentional about the vision and mission of the school.

> The very essence of leadership is . . . vision.
>
> —Theodore Hesburgh

Leaders must cultivate followers. Help them align their personal thinking with school goals. Help them expand their own leadership capacity and do not be afraid to embrace distributed leadership.

Every leader in a school makes a difference, either positive or negative, every day. If legacy is defined as that part of ourselves that we leave with others with whom we come in contact, leaders leave their legacy behind every time they interact with a student. What will that legacy be? The answer to this question determines the success or failure of educational leaders.

The following poem asks a similar question.

The Builder

> I saw a group of men in my hometown.
> I saw a group of men tearing a building down.
> With a heave and a ho and a mighty yell,
> They swung a beam and to the sidewalk fell.
> And I said to the foreman, "Are these men skilled,
> The type you'd hire if you wanted to build?"
> And he laughed and said, "Why no indeed."
> Common labor is all I need.

> For I can tear down in a day or two
> What it took a builder ten years to do.
> And I thought to myself as I walked away,
> Which of these roles am I going to play?
>
> Anonymous but quoted by Lou Holtz (1989)
> *The Fighting Spirit: A Championship Season at Notre Dame*

Which role will you play? Principals who create conversations and generate change around the elements included in this book, should see a better school culture, more motivated teachers, more effort-driven students, and increased student learning.

References and Further Readings

Bernhardt, V. (2003). "Using data to improve student achievement." *Educational Leadership, 60* (5), 26–30.

Bloom, B. (1956). *Taxonomy of educational objectives: Handbook 1. Cognitive domain.* Longman, NY: Longman.

Brown, J. S., Collins, A., & Duguid, P. (1989). "Situated cognition and the culture of learning." *Educational Researcher, 18* (1), 32–42.

Cain, S., & Laird, M. (2011). *The fundamental 5: The formula for quality instruction.* CreateSpace Independent Publishing Platform.

Center for School Change (2013). Downloaded from: http://centerforschoolchange.org/publications/minnesota-charter-school-handbook/vision-and-mission/

Collins, J. (2005). *Good to great and the social sectors.* New York: HarperCollins Publishers.

Covey, S. R. (1990). *The 7 habits of highly effective people.* New York: Free Press.

Covey, S. R. (2012). *The wisdom and teachings of Stephen R. Covey.* New York: Free Press.

Crane, T. G. (2012). *The heart of coaching.* San Diego, CA: FTA Press.

Cranton, P. (2006). *Understanding and promoting transformative learning: A guide for educators of adults* (2nd ed.). San Francisco, CA: John Wiley & Sons, Inc.

DiPaola, M. (2007). *Principals improving instruction: Supervision, evaluation, and professional development.* Boston: Allyn and Bacon.

DuFour, R. (2008). *Revisiting professional learning communities at work: New insights for improving schools.* Bloomington, IL: Solution Tree.

Dunn, R. (1993). *Teaching secondary students through their individual learning styles.* Boston: Allyn and Bacon.

Dweck, C. (2006). *Mindset: The new psychology of success.* New York: Random House.

Elias, M. (2013). "Ethical leadership: Codifying Success." *Principal Leadership, 14* (4), 18–21.

Fullan. M., Hill, P., & Crevola, C. (2006). *Breakthrough.* Thousand Oaks, CA: Corwin Press.

Goffee, R., & Jones, G. (2006). *Why should anyone be led by you?: What it takes to be an authentic leader.* Boston, MA: Harvard Business Press.

Hattie, J. (2011). *Visible learning for teachers: Maximizing impact on learning.* New York: Routledge.

Heath, C., & Heath, D. (2010). *Switch: How to change things when change is hard.* New York: Broadway Books.

Hunter, R. (2004). *Madeline Hunter's mastery teaching: Increasing instructional effectiveness in elementary and secondary schools.* Thousand Oaks, CA: Corwin Press.

Jones, R. E., & Wheeler, G. A. (2011). *The Virginia model: Profiles and common themes.* Richmond, VA: Virginia Foundation for Educational Leadership.

Katzenbach, J., & Smith, D. (2003). *The wisdom of teams.* New York: HarperCollins.

Kelley, R. E. (1992). *The power of followership: How to create leaders people want to follow, and followers who lead themselves.* New York: Doubleday.

King, M. L., Jr. (2010). *Strength to love.* Minneapolis, MN: Fortress Press.

Knight, J. (2013). *High impact instruction: A framework for great teaching.* Thousand Oaks, CA: Corwin Press.

Kotter, J. (2012). *Leading change.* Boston: Harvard Business Review Press.

Kouzes, J. M., & Posner, B. Z. (2010). *The truth about leadership.* San Francisco, CA: Jossey-Bass.

Knowles, M., Holton, E. F., III, & Swanson, R. A. (2008). *The adult learner: The definitive classic in adult education and human resources* (6th ed.). Burlington, MA: Elsevier.

Leithwood, K., & Lewis, K. S. (2012). *Linking leadership to student learning.* San Francisco, CA: Jossey-Bass.

Lewin, K. (1947). "Frontiers in group dynamics: concept, method and reality in social science; social equilibria and social change." *Human Relations* 1(5), downloaded at http://hum.sagepub.com/content/1/1/5.full.pdf+html.

Marzano, R. J. (2001). *Classroom instruction that works.* Alexandria, VA: Association for Supervision and Curriculum Development.

Marzano, R. J. (2003). *What works in schools: Translating research into action.* Alexandria, VA: Association for Supervision and Curriculum Development.

Marzano, R. (2007). *The art and science of teaching: A comprehensive framework for effective instruction.* Alexandria, VA: Association for Supervision and Curriculum Development.

National Association of Secondary School Principals. (2011). *Breaking Ranks®: The Comprehensive Framework for School Improvement.* Reston, VA: National Association of Secondary School Principals.

National Institute of School Leadership. (2013). Website at http://www.nisl.net/.

Ontario Principals Council. (2009). *The principal as mathematics leader.* Thousand Oaks, CA: Corwin Press.

Palestini, R. (2012). *A common sense approach to educational leadership: Lessons from the founders.* Lanham, MD: Rowman & Littlefield.

Partnership for 21st Century Skills (2013). Website at http://www.p21.org/.

Pausch, R. (2008). *The last lecture.* New York: Hyperion.

Pink, D. (2006). *A whole new mind: Why right-brainers will rule the future.* New York: Riverhead Books.

Pink, D. (2010). *Drive: The surprising truth about what motivates us.* New York: Penguin.

Redding, S. (2006). *The mega system: Deciding. Learning. Connecting.* Lincoln, IL: Academic Development Institute.

Reiss, K. (2007). *Leadership coaching for educators.* Thousand Oaks, CA: Corwin Press.

Search Institute. (2013). Website located at http://www.search-institute.org/.

Sizer, T. R. (1999). "No two are quite alike." *Educational Leadership,* 57 (1), 6–11.

Southern Region Education Board. (2010). *The Three Essentials: Improving Schools Requires District Vision, District and State Support, and Principal Leadership.* Downloaded from http://www.wallacefoundation.org/knowledge-center/school-leadership/district-policy-and-practice/Documents/Three-Essentials-to-Improving-Schools.pdf.

Sternberg, R., & Horvath, J. (1995). "A prototype view of expert teaching." *Educational Researcher,* 24 (6), 9–17.

Squire, K. D., & Reigeluch, C. (2000). "The many faces of systemic change." *Educational Horizons,* 78 (3), 143–152.

Tomlinson, C. (2010). *Leading and Managing a Differentiated Classroom.* Alexandria, VA: Association for Supervision and Curriculum Development.

Tough, A. (1971). *The adult's learning projects: A fresh approach to theory and practice in adult learning.* Toronto: OISE.

About the Author

Roger E. Jones is professor and chair of leadership studies at Lynchburg College, Lynchburg, Virginia, where he teaches in both the master's and doctoral programs. He also directs the Virginia Association of Secondary School Principals (VASSP) Center for Educational Leadership which is housed on campus. He is a member of the Virginia Foundation for Educational Leadership (VFEL) faculty and works with schools in improvement. He has completed the Executive Development Program through the National Institute of School Leadership (NISL).

Prior to joining the faculty at Lynchburg College, Jones spent more than thirty years in the Lynchburg, Virginia City Schools as a teacher, coach, middle school principal, high school principal, and assistant superintendent for curriculum and instruction. He was active in VASSP serving in several leadership positions including president.

Jones has degrees from Brevard College (AA), Western Carolina University (BSE), Arkansas State University (MSE), and the University of Virginia (EdD). In 2012, he was inducted into the Gallery of Distinguished Alumni at Brevard College.

www.ingramcontent.com/pod-product-compliance
Lightning Source LLC
Chambersburg PA
CBHW030147240426
43672CB00005B/307